BRITISH AND IRISH AUT

Introductory critical studies

HENRY JAMES

This book introduces school and university students, as well as the interested general reader, to the major novels of Henry James (1843–1916), the American writer who became a great European novelist and died a naturalized Englishman.

The principal novels in which James explored his central theme, the betrayal of innocence, are discussed in a lucid way which offers fresh interpretations and communicates to the non-specialist reader the excitement rather than the difficulty of reading James. Difficulty is nonetheless often a feature of his work, and Judith Woolf does not shun important questions. She places him in the context of the history of the English novel (Fielding, Richardson, Dickens and George Eliot), focusing on traditions of tragic and comic vision and on the subtleties of expression and perspective enabled by the narrative form.

The book includes a short account of James's life, a list of his works and their dates, and a selected guide to further criticism.

BRITISH AND IRISH AUTHORS
Introductory critical studies

In the same series:

Richard Dutton *Ben Jonson: to the first folio*
Robert Wilcher *Andrew Marvell*
David Hopkins *John Dryden*
Jocelyn Harris *Samuel Richardson*
Simon Varey *Henry Fielding*
John Barnard *John Keats*
Elaine Jordan *Alfred Tennyson*
Peter Raby *Oscar Wilde*
John Batchelor *H. G. Wells*
Patrick Parrinder *James Joyce*
John Batchelor *Virginia Woolf*
Martin Scofield *T. S. Eliot: the poems*
Andrew Kennedy *Samuel Beckett*

HENRY JAMES

The major novels

JUDITH WOOLF

Lecturer in the Department of English and Related Literature,
University of York

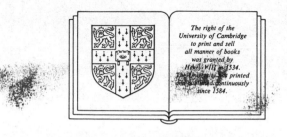

The right of the
University of Cambridge
to print and sell
all manner of books
was granted by
Henry VIII in 1534.
The University has printed
and published continuously
since 1584.

CAMBRIDGE UNIVERSITY PRESS

Cambridge
New York   Port Chester
Melbourne   Sydney

Published by the Press Syndicate of the University of Cambridge
The Pitt Building, Trumpington Street, Cambridge CB2 1RP
40 West 20th Street, New York, NY 10011, USA
10 Stamford Road, Oakleigh, Melbourne 3166, Australia

First published 1991

Printed in Great Britain at the University Press, Cambridge

British Library cataloguing in publication data

Woolf, Judith
Henry James: the major novels.–(British and Irish
authors)
I. Title II. Series
813.4

Library of Congress cataloguing in publication data

Woolf, Judith, 1946–
Henry James: the major novels/Judith Woolf.
p.   cm.--(British and Irish authors)
Includes bibliographical references.
ISBN 0 521 30370 2 (hardback). – ISBN 0 521 31655 3 (paperback)
I. James, Henry, 1843–1916 – Criticism and interpretation.
I. Title.   II. Series.
PS2124 W6 1991
813'.4 – dc20   90–39991
                                                          CIP

ISBN 0 521 30370 2 hardback
ISBN 0 521 31655 3 paperback

UP

For Jacques Berthoud

ὥσπερ ξένοι χαίρουσι πατρίδα βλέπειν,
οὕτως καὶ τοῖς κάμνουσι βιβλίου τέλος.

Contents

Acknowledgements   *page* viii
A brief life of Henry James   ix
Bibliographical note   xii

1 Introduction   1
2 *The Europeans, Washington Square, Daisy Miller*   19
3 *The Portrait of a Lady*   35
4 *The Bostonians*   59
5 *What Maisie Knew*   69
6 *The Awkward Age, The Ambassadors*   83
7 *The Wings of the Dove*   103
8 *The Golden Bowl*   131
9 Afterword   156

Select bibliography   159

Acknowledgements

Among the many friends and colleagues to whom I am indebted, I would particularly like to thank Hazel Beacon, Stephen Minta and Tim Webb for their patience and their illuminating comments, Hugh Haughton for tracing a lost quotation, Bob Jones for reading the manuscript and making many helpful suggestions and Jacques Berthoud for his generous support and encouragement.

A brief life of Henry James

Henry James was born on 15 April 1843 at 21 Washington Place, New York, of Irish and Scots-Irish descent. His grandfather William James had been an immigrant, self-made man and multi-millionaire; his father, Henry James senior, was an unworldly amateur philosopher and Swedenborgian whose ever-changing educational theories led to the young James and his brothers and sister spending their formative years in Europe. The family returned to America in 1858.

When the Civil War broke out in 1861, the question of whether he should volunteer was settled for James when he injured his back while helping to put out a fire, an injury he suffered from intermittently for much of the rest of his life. His two younger brothers, Wilky and Robertson, fought on the Union side, though his elder brother William, later to become the famous philosopher and psychologist, went to study at Lawrence Scientific School at Harvard instead.

In 1869 James returned to Europe and spent a year travelling in England, France and Italy. It was while he was abroad that he heard of the death from tuberculosis of his young cousin Minny Temple, whose fate was later to be the inspiration for two of his greatest novels, *The Portrait of a Lady* and *The Wings of the Dove*. Whether or not he was in love with Minny, James certainly loved her – he was to write many years later that her death felt like the end of youth both for his brother William and himself. Minny's death, together with the destruction of so many young men of his generation in the Civil War, may account for James's life-long preoccupation with the theme of the betrayal of the young and innocent.

In 1876, after trying literary life both in New York and Paris, James settled in London, where he was to be based for most of the rest of his life. In 1878, the publication of *Daisy Miller* brought him the kind of acclaim, both in England and America, that he was never to experience again. The next few years were full of family cares, with the death first of his mother and then of his father in 1882, and of his brother Wilky in 1883, and the arrival in England of his sister Alice in 1884. James had a difficult relationship with Alice, his youngest sibling and only sister, who had reacted to the frustrations of her upbringing – though highly intelligent, she was the only James child whose education was neglected – by relapsing into a life of neurotic invalidism. She died prematurely in 1892, of breast cancer, leaving a *Diary* which shows the literary potential she never had the chance to develop.

In 1890, James embarked on a short-lived flirtation with the theatre, which came to an abrupt end in 1895 when he was booed at the first night of his play *Guy Domville*, a bewildering ordeal for a shy and civilized author. However, he reacted to it bravely; his friend Edmund Gosse, visiting him the next morning, found him breakfasting calmly and proclaiming his satisfaction at having 'escaped for ever from the foul fiend Excision'.

In 1897, James rented Lamb House in Rye, Sussex. This house, which he later bought, became his home for the rest of his life. Though *The Golden Bowl*, his last completed novel, was published in 1904, James continued to write. Between 1906 and 1909 he edited what he saw as his best fiction for the New York edition of *The Novels and Tales of Henry James*, revising his work meticulously and writing copious prefaces. After the death of his brother William in 1910, James began work on a series of autobiographies – presented, modestly, as biographies of William – two of which, *A Small Boy and Others* and *Notes of a Son and Brother*, were completed and published. James was at work on a third volume, *The Middle Years*, when the First World War broke out.

James was devastated by this final evidence of the treachery of life, writing to his friend Howard Sturgis on the day after war was declared:

The plunge of civilization into this abyss of blood and darkness ... is a thing that so gives away the whole long age during which we had supposed the world to be, with whatever abatement, gradually bettering, that to have to take it all now for what the treacherous years were all the while really making for and *meaning* is too tragic for any words.

By now over seventy, he abandoned work on *The Middle Years* and on a final novel, *The Ivory Tower*, to sit by the bedsides of wounded Belgian soldiers, talking to them kindly and simply in his excellent French. In 1915, to express his solidarity with the country he had lived in for so long, he applied for British citizenship.

On 2 December 1915, James suffered the first of a series of strokes which incapacitated him both mentally and physically, though he was lucid enough on New Year's Day 1916 to receive the certificate of the Order of Merit. He died on 28 February 1916, and after a funeral service in Chelsea Old Church his ashes were taken back to America to be buried beside the graves of his family.

Bibliographical note

I have used the New York edition of *The Novels and Tales of Henry James*, Scribner Reprint Editions, re-issued by Augustus M. Kelley by arrangement with Charles Scribner's Sons, 1971–6, for all but the following texts:

The Europeans, from William T. Stafford (ed.), *Henry James: Novels 1871–1880*, Literary Classics of America, Inc. and Cambridge University Press, 1983

Washington Square and *The Bostonians*, from William T. Stafford (ed.), *Henry James: Novels 1881–1886*, Literary Classics of America, Inc. and Cambridge University Press, 1985

Daisy Miller, from Leon Edel (ed.), *The Complete Tales of Henry James*, vol. IV, Rupert Hart-Davis, 1962

Bibliographical details of critical and other works quoted or referred to in this book can be found on page 161.

CHAPTER I

Introduction

Difficulty can create its own difficulties. The initial stumbling-block with Henry James, for many of his readers, is not so much the fact that his novels are complex and oblique and idiosyncratic as a suspicious feeling that such complexity is wilful and unnecessary. This reaction is not, of course, by any means confined to James. Readers frequently approach writers as different from each other as John Donne from James Joyce with the same puzzled suspicion. In some of these difficult writers the difficulties, though necessary, are in a sense wilful, in that they are intended to divert or to delight, to exercise the author's ingenuity and the reader's wits, to astonish or even to tease, though they may have other and profoundly serious aims as well. To complain about this kind of difficulty is like complaining because a riddle is puzzling or because a firework is dazzling. Sterne's *Tristram Shandy*, Pope's *Dunciad*, Joyce's *Ulysses* are all examples of the kind of work I mean. However, there is another kind of difficulty, that of the mathematical expression which is difficult because it formulates precisely a difficult concept which could not otherwise be accurately expressed. To find fitting words for concepts of that order of difficulty but made shifting and changeful as well by all the myriad colourings of human life is a task that imposes its own constraints, all the more so if the truths to be expressed are of overwhelming importance to the writer. In the following chapters I shall try to tease out the complexities and display the virtues of some of James's major works; in this one I want to put James into his context in the history of the English novel, and thus to show him for what he was, a writer using an essentially

I

comic medium to convey an increasingly tragic vision, and so compelled to force the language of narrative prose to carry the charge and register the subtleties of the language of poetry.

Since this is a task which would properly require the whole of a book much longer than this one, the history that I am about to offer you will be a kind of aerial view, enabling us at least to pick out, besides a few of the principal monuments, something of that patterning in the ground which shows the position of ancient forts and fields. Our aerial view, in other words, will take us back in time to the mid-eighteenth century when a middle-aged journalist and lawyer, Henry Fielding, and a middle-aged printer, Samuel Richardson, became, as the old joke tells us, the father and mother of the English novel. The novel, which seems to us so central and traditional, was then that astonishing thing, a brand new literary genre, a kind of prose narrative completely different from the chronicles and romances which preceded it and one still discovering its own scope and powers. Its rise was associated with the rise of a new kind of audience, an educated, largely urban bourgeoisie, deeply interested in its own nature and customs and excited and sometimes shocked to discover them reflected in this new form of literature.

An important forerunner of this new genre was Restoration drama, the sharp, witty comedy, with its accurate caricature of social types and tendencies, which replaced the long-outmoded tragedies of the Jacobeans when the theatres opened again under Charles II. For the first time, the characters on stage mimicked, though with comically wicked exaggeration, the lives and manners of their audience. In Vanbrugh's *The Provok'd Wife*, the two heroines even discuss together the way they behave while watching a play, the joke requiring the half-reluctant laughter of an audience finding itself unexpectedly caught out.

LADY BRUTE: Tell me true – did you never practise in the glass?
BELINDA: Why, did you?
LADY BRUTE: Yes, faith, many a time.
BELINDA: And I too, I own it. Both how to speak myself, and how to look when others speak. But my glass and I could never yet

agree what face I should make when they come blurt out with a
nasty thing in a play. For all the men presently look upon the
women, that's certain; so laugh we must not, though our stays
burst for't, because that's telling truth, and owning we
understand the jest. And to look serious is so dull, when the
whole house is a-laughing.

LADY BRUTE: Besides, that looking serious does really betray our
knowledge in the matter, as much as laughing with the company
would do. For if we did not understand the thing, we should
naturally do like other people.

BELINDA: For my part I always take that occasion to blow my nose.

LADY BRUTE: You must blow your nose half off then at some plays.

(Act III Sc. 3)

It is no accident that Fielding began his literary career as a
dramatist. His greatest novel, *Tom Jones*, is a kind of exuberant
puppet show with Fielding himself entering the novel as the
cunning puppet-master who speaks to the audience from inside
his booth, inducing us to enter into an intimate relationship
with him. This close but teasing relationship between author
and reader is sharply contrasted with the relationships of the
characters themselves. Fielding has a serious moral purpose in
writing his novel, but none of the characters change in the
course of it, any more than they would in a fairy-tale. Tom, the
foundling hero, simply turns out to have been all along a true
member of his benefactor's family, as well as a good lad at
heart, while Master Blifil, his rival and enemy, turns out to
have been all along a hypocrite. People are not always what
they seem, at least to the other characters, who are denied the
Olympian insights the author shares with the reader, but they
are always what they look like. Tom's handsome face
guarantees his good heart. As in a fairy-tale, too, we can rely on
the happy ending, though it may be as hard to see how Fielding
is going to extract it from the ever more inextricable tangles of
the plot as to see how the conjurer is going to turn the white
rabbit back into the young lady assistant he earlier had sawn
in half. When Oedipus discovers that he has unwittingly lain
with his own mother his predicament is the archetypal stuff of
tragedy and we shudder at it. When Tom Jones appears to
have discovered that he has done the same thing our reaction

is more like 'oops!' though perhaps an edge of ancient horror
sharpens our laughter when she turns out not to have been his
mother after all.

The tension between the puppet-like simplicity of the
characters, the comic complexities of the plot and the projection
of the author, and through him the cajoled and flattered and
partly invented reader, into the novel itself is maintained
through an alert and constantly shifting prose which runs
through a range of parodic effects. There is room here for only
one example, the introduction of the heroine Sophia Western at
the beginning of Book iv. Fielding pauses, before ushering her
in, to deliver a little lecture on 'similes, descriptions, and other
kind of poetical embellishments', which serve the same purpose
as civic processions or fanfares in the theatre, giving an illusion
of importance to what follows them.

When I have seen a man strutting in a procession, after others whose
business hath been only to walk before him, I have conceived a higher
notion of his dignity, than I have felt on seeing him in a common
situation.

We are at the back of the puppet-booth being told how the next
trick is going to work before Fielding rolls up his sleeves and
begins:

And now, without any further preface, we proceed to our next
chapter.

Chapter 2
A short Hint of what we can do in the Sublime, and
a Description of Miss Sophia Western

Hushed be every ruder breath. May the heathen ruler of the winds
confine in iron chains the boisterous limbs of noisy Boreas, and the
sharp-pointed nose of bitter-biting Eurus. Do thou, sweet Zephyrus,
rising from thy fragrant bed, mount the western sky, and lead on
those delicious gales, the charms of which call forth the lovely Flora
from her chamber, perfumed with pearly dews, when on the first of
June, her birthday, the blooming maid, in loose attire, gently trips it
over the verdant mead, where every flower rises to do her homage, 'til
the whole field becomes enamelled, and colours contend with sweets
which shall ravish her most.

So charming may she now appear; and you the feather'd choristers
of nature, whose sweetest notes not even Handel can excel, tune your
melodious throats, to celebrate her appearance.

Mock-sublime gives way to mock-realism when Sophia is finally described:

Sophia then, the only daughter of Mr Western, was a middle-sized woman; but rather inclining to tall.

However, that deflating first sentence is followed by a detailed account of her beauties, barely tempered by minor criticisms and embellished by quotations from Suckling and Donne. By the time we reach the description of her breasts (which Fielding refuses to mention by name for fear of making his puppet blush) and learn that:

Here was whiteness which no lillies, ivory, nor alabaster could match. The finest cambric might indeed be supposed from envy to cover that bosom, which was much whiter than itself

we are back in the eulogizing world of the Elizabethan sonneteers, and Fielding has pulled off his trick. He has ushered in his heroine with 'poetical embellishments' and induced us to swallow them in spite of being forewarned; and now, after making the essential fairy-tale point that Sophia is as good as she is beautiful, he can put her back in the puppet-booth and let the show go on.

Fielding, it will be clear by now, is one of the riddling and dazzling writers, though his art is presented as artlessness; Richardson, though his greatest novel, *Clarissa*, is even more of a technical *tour de force* than *Tom Jones*, writes under the compulsion of his subject-matter. His first novel, *Pamela*, the story of a virtuous servant-girl who turns the tables on the master, who imprisons and attempts to seduce her, by ending up as his wife, is trivialized by the drive of the novel as a genre towards the happy ending. It was the urge to expose what he saw as Pamela's hypocrisy which led Fielding to write first *Shamela* and then *Joseph Andrews*, and so to become a novelist; and the lesson of *Shamela* was not lost on Richardson. In *Clarissa* he retells the story of Pamela and makes of it the first great tragic novel to be written in the English language.

This is a novel as unlike *Tom Jones* as can well be imagined. It consists of a long-drawn-out and terrifying duel between a

clever, rather priggish but essentially inexperienced girl and a
compulsive seducer who becomes obsessed by the challenge she
presents as the one woman he is unable to subdue and thus
unable to leave. The pressure of this obsession builds up in
Lovelace to the point where he drugs Clarissa and then rapes
her in front of the prostitutes in the brothel where he has
imprisoned her, only to find that, possessing her in this way, he
has not possessed her at all. He has broken the girl herself
without breaking the thing that opposes him – her will. She
escapes him irrevocably into death and he is left raving of how
he has loved her, the 'pearl of great price' for whom he has
paid so much.

Her dear heart and a lock of her hair I will have, let who will be the
gainsayers! For is she not mine? Whose else can she be? She has no
father nor mother, no sister, no brother; no relations but me. And my
beloved is mine; and I am hers: and that's enough – but oh!

> She's out! The damp of death has quench'd
>   her quite!
> Those spicy doors, her lips, are shut, close
>   lock'd,
> Which never gale of life shall open more!   (letter 497)

Where Fielding's characters were free to ramble and pursue
each other across England, meeting with picaresque adventures
on the way, Richardson forces Clarissa into narrower and
narrower confinements until all that is left to her is a coffin. It
is an airless and claustrophobic world he conjures up, all the
more so as the protagonists here are not puppets but fully
developed and psychologically complex human beings trapped
in a situation whose inexorable logic drives them always deeper
in until they reach the smallest box of all at the centre of the
maze. The means Richardson uses to achieve this effect are
curious ones to the modern reader. It will be obvious by now
that *Clarissa*, despite its interest in the morality of the
contemporary bourgeoisie, owes more to Shakespearian
tragedy than it does to Restoration comedy, but its technique
derives from a more primitive form of the novel itself, the fiction-
as-documentary of Defoe, who presented Moll Flanders and

Robinson Crusoe to his readers as real-life case-histories. What Richardson gives us is the documents in the case, in the form of two voluminous collections of letters, one between Clarissa and her feminist friend Anna Howe and the other between Lovelace and his crony Belford, a more shrinking rake and eventually a repentant one. This handing over of the task of writing the novel to the characters themselves has several important consequences. Since we always learn of events just after they have happened, the novel gains a kind of retarded immediacy which helps to build up our anxiety for the heroine and which also adds a marvellously unexpected *frisson* to the description of Clarissa's death-bed as we suddenly realize that even as we seem to watch her dying she is already dead. It goes without saying that we gain a detailed insight into the minds of the characters; more important is the sense, illusory but powerful, that we have direct access to those minds. Richardson's technique makes him invisible, and the apparent absence of a controlling author pulling the strings makes the unstoppable nature of the tragedy more appalling, though it also left Richardson with no recourse but anxious footnotes when the earliest readers, failing to recognize the psychotic nature of Lovelace's obsession, persisted in falling in love with him.

As with Fielding's method in *Tom Jones*, the success of *Clarissa* depends on the richness and variety of the language, though here that language is mimetic, like the language of the playwright who must persuade us that it is not Shakespeare but Iago or Desdemona who speaks. Again there is space for only one example. Here, Clarissa, crazy with the after-effect of the drug and the discovery that she has been raped, writes piteously to Lovelace:

Oh Lovelace! if you could be sorry for yourself, I would be sorry too – but when all my doors are fast, and nothing but the keyhole open, and the key of late put into that, to be where you are, in a manner without opening any of them – O wretched, wretched Clarissa Harlowe!

For I never will be Lovelace – let my uncle take it as he pleases.

Well, but now I remember what I was going to say...

Alas! you have killed my head among you – I don't say who did it

– God forgive you all! – But had it not been better to have put me out
of all your ways at once? You might safely have done it! For nobody
would require me at your hands – no, not a soul – except, indeed,
Miss Howe would have said, when she should see you, What,
Lovelace, have you done with Clarissa Harlowe? And then you could
have given any slight gay answer – Sent her beyond sea; or, She has
run away from me as she did from her parents. And this would have
been easily credited; for you know, Lovelace, she that could run away
from *them*, might very well run away from *you*.
    But this is nothing to what I wanted to say.   (letter 261.1)

    This is prose of an almost Shakespearian subtlety, very
different from the passage we examined from *Tom Jones* where
the language had a fine comic sweep which aimed at bold and
sharply contrasted effects. The Freudian imagery with which
Clarissa gropes, in her drug-induced confusion, towards the
almost ungraspable horror of sexual violation,

but when all my doors are fast, and nothing but the keyhole open,
and the key of late put into that...

the equation of rape with murder in the double connotations of
that haunting question, 'What, Lovelace, have you done with
Clarissa Harlowe?' the echo of *Othello* ('She has deceived her
father, and may thee') which establishes Clarissa as a modern
Desdemona, are all achieved without any sacrifice of natu-
ralness. We feel as we read that it is not the conscious mind of
Richardson but the subconscious mind of Clarissa herself which
is making these connections and allusions. It will be evident by
now that it is from Clarissa Harlowe and not from Sophia
Western that Isabel Archer and Milly Theale take their
descent.
    This contrast between possible models, the comic novel with
its obtrusive author manipulating his cast of puppets and the
tragic novel with its apparently absent author superseded by
his characters, presented the novelists of the nineteenth century
with a challenge and a choice. (I am here omitting Sterne, who
was one of the ancestors of modernism and whose methods and
inventions were only really taken up again at the start of the
present century.) There was a challenge, too, in what these
earlier novelists failed to do. Fielding and Richardson were

alike in writing big discursive novels with no very tight organizing principle; Fielding because he wanted to preserve the spontaneity and freedom of the picaresque narrative, Richardson because of the scope the epistolary method gave him for minutely detailed investigations into the psychology of his characters, but also both of them because the idea of a tightly organized novel had not yet been invented. The development of a narrative technique which combined a new degree of formal control with a flawless appearance of naturalism was the striking achievement of Jane Austen, though it was an achievement bought at a price which makes her work something of a cul-de-sac in the history of the English novel. Where her immediate predecessors Fanny Burney and Maria Edgeworth had felt free to draw on a range of human experience wide enough to include blackmail, suicide, abduction, lesbianism and breast cancer, Jane Austen can admit no material more dangerous than accidents, elopements, misunderstandings and unfulfilled bad intentions. She submits so completely to the tendency in the novel to seek the happy ending that she can even use its inevitability to tease her readers:

The anxiety, which in this state of their attachment must be the portion of Henry and Catherine, and of all who loved either, as to its final event, can hardly extend, I fear, to the bosom of my readers, who will see in the tell-tale compression of the pages before them, that we are all hastening together to perfect felicity.

(*Northanger Abbey* ch. 16)

Though that sentence in itself is enough to display Jane Austen, despite the narrow compass of her material, as a highly sophisticated writer, she does not demand an answering sophistication in her readers, providing as she does a homogeneous moral universe in which we are unobtrusively guided to the correct solution to all moral problems – Emma is wrong to be rude to Miss Bates; Fanny Price is right to refuse Henry Crawford; Anne Elliot, tricky case, was correct to follow Lady Russell's advice to break off her engagement, but Lady Russell was injudicious in offering it. This deftly unobtrusive provision

of an internally consistent world full, as the real world is not, of
moral certainties may at least partly explain the appeal of her
novels to people who do not otherwise read imaginative
literature at all, like the First World War soldiers in Kipling's
short story 'The Janeites' whose shared game of joking
references to the novels opposes a fragile barrier of civilization
to the nightmare actuality which surrounds them and in which
most of them eventually die. 'There's no one to touch Jane
when you're in a tight place', exclaims one of them at the end
of the tale. 'Gawd bless 'er, whoever she was.'

Jane Austen, in other words, is not a difficult writer – or not
until we pause to consider how she brings off her effects. For
Henry James, in whose later novels those confident moral
values of Highbury and Mansfield Park shimmer and dis-
integrate, the notion that 'the tell-tale compression of the
pages' must promise the arrival of 'perfect felicity' is one he
strains at in *The Europeans* and has already completely subverted
by the time he writes *Washington Square*, almost an anti-version
of *Persuasion* with the exemplary patience of the heroine
rewarded only with a final twist of the knife. James's business
with Jane Austen (or rather, with an idea of the novel of which
her work is the crystallization) is finished early, leaving him to
take up more directly the challenge offered by those great
Victorian successors to Fielding and Richardson, Dickens and
George Eliot.

Dickens, like Fielding, is the novelist as puppet-master. Once
again we have the wide-ranging, capacious narrative controlled
and dominated by the distinctive voice of the author, once
again we have the cast of marionettes; but where Fielding's
puppets were stereotypes – the ne'er-do-well with a heart of
gold, the sanctimonious hypocrite, the beautiful young girl –
Dickens's puppets are grotesques. The Sophia-figure is still
there but she has become a pallid wax doll, Florence Dombey
or Ada Clare, whose human proportions make her look almost
like a freak among the misshapen creatures that surround her.
The wide landscapes of Fielding's England are still there, but
they have become shrouded and ominous. Fog in the streets of
London, mist on the Essex marshes, smoke from the factory

chimneys of Coketown make an atmosphere as claustrophobic as the air of the locked rooms which imprisoned Clarissa Harlowe. Dickens is the puppet-master, the family entertainer, but these are puppets that bleed. A qualified version of the happy ending is still current, but only for those characters who have not died of smallpox or despair, by fire or railway accidents or spontaneous combustion.

That last preposterous fatality happens to old Krook, the rag-and-bone dealer in *Bleak House*. Let us visit the scene of the death. Two insignificant lawyer's clerks, Mr Weevle (alias Jobling) and Mr Guppy, are waiting together late at night in a room above the rag-and-bone shop, a room where a man has died. They are waiting for the stroke of midnight, when Krook is to hand over to one of them a packet of letters which had belonged to the dead man. They don't yet know (neither does the reader) what has happened to Krook downstairs, but the room is full of soot which smears when it is touched 'like black fat', and Mr Weevle has the horrors without knowing why, and there is a rancid smell in the air. Finally they open the window and make a very unpleasant discovery:

Mr Guppy sitting on the window-sill, nodding his head and balancing all these possibilities in his mind, continues thoughtfully to tap it, and clasp it, and measure it with his hand, until he hastily draws his hand away.

'What in the Devil's name,' he says, 'is this! Look at my fingers!'

A thick, yellow liquor defiles them, which is offensive to the touch and sight and more offensive to the smell. A stagnant, sickening oil, with some natural repulsion in it that makes them both shudder.

'What have you been doing here? What have you been pouring out of window?'

'I pouring out of window! Nothing, I swear! Never, since I have been here!' cries the lodger.

And yet look here – and look here! When he brings the candle, here, from the corner of the window-sill, it slowly drips, and creeps away down the bricks; here, lies in a little thick nauseous pool.

'This is a horrible house,' says Mr Guppy, shutting down the window. 'Give me some water, or I shall cut my hand off.'

He so washes, and rubs, and scrubs, and smells, and washes, that he has not long restored himself with a glass of brandy, and stood silently before the fire, when Saint Paul's bell strikes twelve, and all

Introduction

those other bells strike twelve from their towers of various heights in
the dark air and in their many tones. When all is quiet again, the
lodger says:

'It's the appointed time at last. Shall I go?'

Mr Guppy nods, and gives him a 'lucky touch' on the back; but
not with the washed hand, though it is his right hand.   (ch. 32)

The mixture of artifice and realism in this passage creates a
curious and rather sinister effect. The two clerks have already
been established as minor comic characters, mere gargoyles on
the huge edifice of the novel, and the event which occasions
their horrible discovery, the death by spontaneous combustion
of the old rag-and-bone dealer, is perhaps as improbable a
happening (despite its origin in newspaper accounts of baffling
fatalities) as any novelist has ever tried to make actual; but the
'thick, yellow liquor' on the window-sill, that *is* real. The feel
and the sight and the smell of it rise off the page at us, to be
troublingly supplanted by another kind of reality, which can
only be described as the reality of poetry, when all the bells
strike twelve 'from their towers of various heights in the dark
air'. As we take in this sombre and beautiful image, a couple of
strings, a couple of instinctive reflexes, twitch in one of the
puppets. Mr Guppy gives his companion a 'lucky touch' on the
back. We recognize the deep source that generates this impulse
– it is something that we share with Mr Guppy – but it is the
other impulse modifying the gesture that really makes us
shudder. Mr Guppy is impelled to touch his friend, 'but not
with the washed hand, though it is his right hand'. The realism
with which Dickens has evoked the contaminating substance
on the window-sill now acts to make us understand from the
inside the constraints on Guppy's little gesture. The puppet
suddenly glances at us with a human face, or perhaps, since it
is a grotesque (even, strictly speaking, an impossible) reality
which has created this moment of insight, we discover ourselves
to be partly puppets.

Though Dickens is undoubtedly a novelist in the tradition of
Fielding, the subtleties of language in this passage recall that
other tradition which began with Richardson. The comic
novelist, in other words, is here making use, for his own ends,

of the poetic resources of the tragic novel. James may have
learnt the elegance of controlled form from Jane Austen, but
perhaps it was partly from Dickens that he learnt a truth that
precedes and controls form, the realization of how close, in the
possibilities open to the novel, poetry may lie to the grotesque
and to the mundane. However, it is to George Eliot that James
owes his greatest debt. So strong was her influence that he can
be seen as the connecting link between her novel of conscience
and the novel of consciousness as it appears in the early
twentieth century in the work of Proust or Joyce. We have seen
how Dickens perverted the tradition of Fielding in the direction
of poetry. It could be said of George Eliot that she perverted the
tradition of Richardson in the direction of prose, and to
understand her influence on James we must examine the effects
of this on her novels.

George Eliot is pre-eminently the novelist of moral choice
and in this she differs sharply from Richardson, though
inheriting from him a conception of the possible scope and
seriousness of the genre. *Clarissa* is an intensely moral book, but
after the initial errors and misunderstandings which put her
into Lovelace's power the only choice open to its heroine is the
choice to say no, to preserve her selfhood by continuing to
oppose the violation she cannot prevent. She is bound by the
inexorability of the tragic action which makes her very integrity
the cause of her destruction. George Eliot lacks the fatalism of
the tragic imagination; she is a believer in free will, with a
strong recognition of the weight of responsibility which this
places on the individual. Her method as a novelist is objective,
almost scientific. Interested above all in how moral choices are
made, she creates in her novels the experimental conditions
under which the process can be studied. These choices, unlike
those facing Jane Austen's characters, are not confined to the
field of personal relationships; George Eliot is as much
concerned with the passions of the intellect, the steady
faithfulness of a man wedded to his trade, the frustrations or the
retreat into cold frivolity which society imposes upon women
when it denies them meaningful work. Here is the boy Lydgate
in *Middlemarch* opening a dusty volume of an old cyclopaedia

on a rainy day and making a discovery which is to shape his
future life:

> The page he opened on was under the heading of Anatomy, and the
> first passage that drew his eyes was on the valves of the heart. He was
> not much acquainted with valves of any sort, but he knew that *valvae*
> were folding doors, and through this crevice came a sudden light
> startling him with his first vivid notion of finely adjusted mechanism
> in the human frame. A liberal education had of course left him free
> to read the indecent passages in the school classics, but beyond a
> general sense of secrecy and obscenity in connection with his internal
> structure, had left his imagination quite unbiassed, so that for
> anything he knew his brains lay in small bags at his temples, and he
> had no more thought of representing to himself how his blood
> circulated than how paper served instead of gold. But the moment of
> vocation had come, and before he got down from his chair, the world
> was made new to him by a presentiment of endless processes filling the
> vast spaces planked out of his sight by that wordy ignorance which he
> had supposed to be knowledge.   (Bk II ch. 15)

This passage, like the book that it comes from, displays a
kind of realism which is new to the English novel. Lydgate, like
Richardson's characters, is being presented to us as a complete
human being, but complete not because his mind contains a
rich and dangerous hinterland of terrors and desires but
because of his capacity for reasoned abstract thought. The key
to the passage is the final word 'knowledge'. Because of her
belief in the responsibility imposed on us by free will, George
Eliot sees moral awareness as a skill that must be learnt, and she
uses learning in its academic sense as a moral metaphor.
Lydgate is culpable because he fails to take the same care over
choosing a wife as he would take over completing a piece of
research. Fred Vincy demonstrates his moral silliness by
cultivating 'gentlemanly' unreadable handwriting, and his
moral re-education involves literally going back to pothooks.

> 'What can I do, Mr Garth?' said Fred, whose spirits had sunk very
> low, not only at the estimate of his handwriting, but at the vision of
> himself as liable to be ranked with office-clerks.
> 'Do? Why, you must learn to form your letters and keep the line.
> What's the use of writing at all if nobody can understand it?'
>   (Bk VI ch. 56)

This emphasis on education involves the reader too. George Eliot is continually appealing to our common experience, confident that we will find that it backs up the moral lessons that her novels teach us. These are not simple lessons. They involve the study of complex human beings operating in equally complex societies (it is not for nothing that she equates the young Lydgate's ignorance of anatomy with his ignorance of economics). In demonstrating the workings of these societies George Eliot contrives to put us on a level with her characters, depriving us of that superior over-view which enabled us to catch out Jane Austen's Emma as she played at dolls with poor Harriet Smith, and reminding us sharply that there are some problems which have no good solutions. Neither Dorothea Brooke nor Gwendolen Harleth can be rescued from their predicaments by a Mr Knightley figure and a marriage and a happy-ever-after. In George Eliot's novels, as in the majority of adult lives, the real problems *begin* with marriage.

All this makes for a new kind of seriousness in the novel just as it makes for a new kind of realism, but these towering achievements are gained at a cost, and the price, as I suggested earlier, is the loss of the tragic consciousness and with it of poetry. The novels assert a norm, demand a commonly intelligible moral language ('What's the use of writing at all if nobody can understand it?'), leave unexplored that dangerous substratum into which Richardson burrowed, neglect dreams, disbelieve in ghosts, defy augury. It is not surprising that the novel which exerted the greatest influence on James, *Daniel Deronda*, is the one in which George Eliot tried, with only partial success, to transcend these limitations. I shall be exploring that influence in detail in the chapter on *The Portrait of a Lady*; at present I want to suggest some of the reasons why the challenge presented by George Eliot's novels pushed James towards an ever greater complexity.

Those novels assert that moral awareness can and must be learnt. For James, equally concerned with moral awareness, it is a matter not so much of learning as of seeing, though seeing too is a skill that must be learnt. His typical metaphor is the analogous activity of looking at a work of art. It is this, and not élitism or aestheticism, which makes art such an important value in the novels. Milly confronting the Bronzino, Strether watching a boat with a pink parasol drifting downstream, experience moments of awareness that are both terrible (what they see is the imminence of death and betrayal) and necessary because they involve the stripping away of illusions. Such moments come unsought and ambush the beholder, and eyes thus opened see all their past experience take on a pattern which is both new and inevitable, since all along it has lain beneath the false appearances of things.

It is this that makes innocence such an ambiguous and troubling concept for James (as indeed it was for Richardson). In novel after novel he explores the incompatibility of innocence and moral awareness. To be truly innocent is to be ignorant of the possibility of being otherwise, but that in itself is a source of danger. Life will either surprise that innocence, forcing it horribly into awareness as the trap closes on it, or else will fail to do so, leaving it untouched and unaware, and thus not really alive. It is a hard fate to be Isabel Archer, but perhaps it is still worse to be Strether, the ageing moral virgin earnestly advising younger men to seize the life that he himself has missed. Yet to exchange innocence for knowledge is not to free oneself from danger. James makes the point very vividly in that passage in *The Awkward Age* where Mr Longdon compares Nanda with the artificially cloistered little Aggie.

Both the girls struck him as lambs with the great shambles of life in their future; but while one, with its neck in a pink ribbon, had no consciousness but that of being fed from the hand with the small sweet biscuit of unobjectionable knowledge, the other struggled with instincts and forebodings, with the suspicion of its doom and the far-borne scent, in the flowery fields, of blood.   (Bk v ch. 3)

In George Eliot's novels the deal meted out by life is often rough justice, but it remains justice of a sort. In *Middlemarch* we get what is almost a social scientist's version of the happy ending. Fred Vincy gets off lightly, Lydgate pays dear, Dorothea does as well as anyone can expect to in an imperfect world, and yet:

Many who knew her, thought it a pity that so substantive and rare
a creature should have been absorbed into the life of another, and
only be known in a certain circle as a wife and mother. But no-one
stated exactly what else that was in her power she ought rather to
have done.   (Finale)

The characters shape their own fates within the bounds of the
possible. James's characters struggle to do this too, but in the
civilized drawing-room as in the flowery fields of Mr Longdon's
imagination, in Maisie's schoolroom, in Regent's Park and the
National Gallery we sense that far-borne scent of blood. In
novel after novel, the lamb, whether or not visited by
forebodings, gazes up at the butcher with love. Catherine
Sloper with Morris Townsend, Isabel Archer with Gilbert
Osmond, Milly Theale with Merton Densher, the doomed girls
choose their partners in the great game of deception and
betrayal. It is a subject-matter which presents a daunting
technical challenge. James must maintain the civilized surface
unflawed even while he gradually reveals what lies beneath it
both in the way of hidden motive and intention and in the way
of 'instincts and forebodings'. He must show us how and why
the betrayer deceives the victim, but also how and why both
betrayer and victim deceive themselves. Compelled by a tragic
vision which admits both the grotesque and the mundane, he
must use all the resources of comedy to sharpen the edge of the
knife.

   It is these constraints, along with James's ever-deepening
sense of the ironies implicit in the duel between innocence and
corruption, which make the novels increasingly complex, and
this complexity takes two different and opposite forms. From
The Portrait of a Lady onwards James conveys much of his
meaning through elaborate patterning and plotting. The comic
symmetries of *What Maisie Knew*, which develop towards the
end of the novel into a kind of dance in which Maisie is pushed
from partner to partner; the network of motivation in *The
Wings of the Dove* which leads every female character in the
novel to join in smoothing the way for Densher to propose to
Milly while preventing all of them from explaining to him what
hey are up to; the pattern of relationships, at once interlocking

and mutually excluding, in *The Golden Bowl* which makes the novel into a kind of Chinese egg or impossible object; all these are ways of conveying the complexities of a moral dilemma. At another level, James explores those complexities through a detailed attention to the process of consciousness in his characters. Plot and technique come together here; as the betrayer gropes his way towards betrayal, blind as the victim to where it will end, James must blindfold the reader too until the moment of vision comes. Both that blindfold progress through the hidden places of the mind and the moment of vision which succeeds it point us on towards the innovations of the twentieth-century novelists, just as the patterning which contains those perceptions points us back beyond the origins of the novel to Shakespearian comedy and Shakespearian tragedy.

Reading James, we join the dance with Maisie. Recognizing, a split second before poor Strether, the owner of the pink parasol, we feel a pleasure that equals his dismay, and yet we understand and share that dismay. Confronting the Bronzino with Milly, we see great art mirroring great art and face death for a moment in that mirror, without fear but with a real shiver. These are the rewards that James offers the attentive reader, and he requires our attentiveness not only because his novels are difficult but because attentiveness itself, imaginative clear vision, is the quality that they ultimately affirm.

The Europeans, Washington Square, Daisy Miller

The betrayal of innocence, then, that central theme of James's major novels, is to be the subject of this book; but we must begin our exploration of it before James himself fully realized and was possessed by his subject-matter, in the early, sunny world of *The Europeans*. This is almost the last novel in which James was to allow his readers the satisfaction of a happy ending, and, remembering Jane Austen's 'perfect felicity', we will not be surprised to find that its hero is called Felix Young. He and his sister Eugenia, the Baroness Münster, are the Europeans of the title: Felix the embodiment of lighthearted youthfulness and his sister, who describes herself as being sometimes a thousand years old, the classic 'older woman' of European fiction, worldly, fascinating and mendacious. Neither of them, of course, is really European in origin. They are the children of a couple of expatriate Americans, reared in Europe and steeped in its values but now returning to their native country hard up and on the make. To be European, we see, is a matter not of nationality but of culture, and it is from the encounter between mutually non-comprehending cultures that the comedy in the novel springs.

Felix and Eugenia have come to America with a common aim but very different attitudes. Felix is unabashedly a tourist, finding, as tourists do, the charm of the foreign in the most mundane details of New England life, even the coke fire in their Boston lodgings:

'Those little blue tongues, dancing on top of the crimson embers, are extremely picturesque. They are like a fire in an alchemist's laboratory.'
(ch. 1)

Eugenia, on the contrary, feels herself to be a woman forced into exile among savages. The sight of a tram-queue of dowdy women all clutching satchels and parcels strikes her not as evidence of the emancipation of the American woman (in *The Bostonians* Verena Tarrant and Miss Birdseye are to join that queue) but simply as a barbarism, and on a walk in the park, while Felix admires the pretty girls, she deplores the lack of older women and of the carriages in which such women should properly be displayed, rolling 'past a hedge of pedestrians, holding their parasols askance'.

It is in analogous ways that the brother and sister respond to their New England cousins, Felix with an observant interest in which the clear-sightedness of an outsider combines with the misinterpretations of a foreigner to give the Wentworths back an image of themselves which causes them perceptible shock, Eugenia determined to think and behave as if her idea of 'civilized' manners were universal, and experiencing surprise and irritation whenever this proves not to be the case. This contrast is in fact based on a similarity; they both read the world in terms of the ambiguities of their own status. Felix is an artist, as his sister is a Baroness, only between inverted commas. The happiness of his nature extends to a gift for a 'happy' likeness, one that flatters the sitter but not so grossly that he fails to accept it as an image of himself. Felix sees only a happy likeness of the world and has a talent for communicating that vision. He is essentially a simplifier. Eugenia, by contrast, is a complicater, an embellisher of life with drapes and flounces. Neither aristocrat nor *demi-mondaine*, though uniting aspects of both, she had had the short-sighted shrewdness as a young girl to sell her virtue for a semi-worthless marriage and title. Longer-sighted now at thirty-three, she is calculating how best to turn to her own advantage her clever brother-in-law's desire that her stupid husband should repudiate the marriage. It is not her own scheming but her underlying feeling of failure and thwarted ambition that she is trying to cover up with silk shawls and old lace.

The Wentworths, until the arrival of these disconcerting cousins, have lived a life without drapes or deceptions, but their transparent honesty is accompanied by a Calvinist moral anxiety which prevents them from ever living on comfortable terms with their own goodness. Felix, unused to the puritan cast of mind, deduces on first meeting them that 'there is something the matter with them; they have some melancholy memory or some depressing expectation'. In a sense he is right. Though they have tempered the religious beliefs of their puritan forebears – they are now Unitarians – the Wentworths still remember the Fall of Man and look forward to the Judgment Day. Despite the innocence of their personal lives, they are pervasively aware of original sin and the need to be constantly on guard against its most trivial manifestations. Felix, with his sunny conviction that he is sinless and his certainty that pleasure is the supreme good, and Eugenia, for whom lies are a civilized social convenience and lying a graceful social skill, enter the Wentworths' house like snakes slipping into a post-lapsarian Eden. To them that house is 'a magnified Nüremberg toy', a big wooden doll's house, and they at once begin to play with the inhabitants.

In the event they prove to be harmless snakes. Eugenia sets her sights on Robert Acton, a wealthy man and the nearest thing to a worldly one that the Wentworth circle offers, but, in an attempt to counter the ennui induced by the simplicities of American life, she also decides to undertake the sentimental education of the Wentworth son Clifford. Clifford is, in his modest way, the black sheep of the family, having been suspended from Harvard because, as his father anxiously tells Felix, 'he was too fond of something of which he should not have been fond. I suppose it is considered a pleasure.' Felix puts a more sophisticated interpretation on this than the facts turn out to warrant; Clifford has merely got drunk. To his father this is a serious moral failing; to Felix it is 'not a vice for a gentleman' and he prescribes a course of Eugenia's company:

'Clifford ought to frequent some agreeable woman, who, without ever mentioning such unsavoury subjects, would give him a sense of its being very ridiculous to be fuddled. If he could fall in love with her a little, so much the better. The thing would operate as a cure.'

(ch. 7)

This ingenious plan fails completely, both because Clifford belongs to a society which sees young girls, like Robert Acton's sister Lizzie, as the only possible sexual objects for a young man to admire and pursue and because he is in any case too stupid to work out what Eugenia is driving at. Worse, the unnecessary complication of Clifford causes Eugenia to expose herself to Robert Acton as a liar and schemer and, worse still, as an incompetent one. She has already noticed him catching her out in a piece of gushing insincerity when she assures his invalid mother that the reticent Acton has talked of her 'immensely'. Her reaction on that occasion was one of righteous indignation: 'but who were these people to whom such fibbing was not pleasing?' However, when Clifford, 'blushing and looking rather awkward', bursts in from where Eugenia has hidden him in Felix's studio, breaking up what Acton has taken to be a private tête-à-tête, not all Eugenia's ingenuity can conceal the fact that the sophisticated drama she has been busily scripting has suddenly degenerated into farce. She is sufficiently affronted to give up a pursuit which has never been more than half-hearted either on her side or on Acton's and returns to Europe, writing off the whole of the 'provincial continent' of America as 'not favourable to really superior women'.

All this is pure comedy and it is only hindsight that alerts the reader to the Baroness's later metamorphoses as Madame Merle and Madame de Vionnet. Neither Acton nor the blushing and awkward Clifford are in any sense Eugenia's victims. However, Felix's part of the story, even though his is the part with the happy ending, is more suggestive of later developments. There is a sense in which *The Europeans* is James's *Pamela*, a comic trial-run for a tragic novel, but if Gertrude Wentworth, like Pamela herself, is a tragic heroine in embryo, she belongs not to Richardson's world but to Hawthorne's, or rather to Hawthorne's world as it might have appeared through the eyes of Jane Austen. We meet her for the first time walking in a peaceful and ordered garden, its 'flowering shrubs' and 'neatly-disposed plants' separated from the 'muddy road', while a church bell rings in the distance. She is an 'innocent sabbath-breaker', an Eve in the Wentworths' post-lapsarian Eden, and the description of her which follows sounds a warning note; almost, in the light of James's later novels, an unfulfilled premonition:

She was tall and pale, thin and a little awkward; her hair was fair and perfectly straight; her eyes were dark, and they had the singularity of seeming at once dull and restless – differing herein, as you see, fatally from the ideal 'fine eyes', which we always imagine to be both brilliant and tranquil.   (ch. 2)

In this respect she differs too from her sister Charlotte, who joins her in the garden. 'Her eyes, unlike the other's, were quick and bright; but they were not at all restless.' Charlotte is wholly at ease with the social and moral ideas of New England and of her own family, ideas which appear to her to be both natural and inevitable but which stir Gertrude to an inarticulate and unfocused rebellion. James's word 'fatally' here is to prove a false alarm as far as Gertrude herself goes; later on Isabel Archer and Milly Theale will really experience what it means to 'differ fatally'.

This particular phrase may be significant only by hindsight. What is certainly no accident is that Gertrude and Charlotte begin almost at once to talk about the right way to wear 'a long, red, India scarf'.

'How should I wear it, dear?'
'I don't know; differently from that. You should draw it differently over your shoulders, round your elbows; you should look differently behind.'
'How should I look?' Charlotte inquired.
'I don't think I can tell you,' said Gertrude, plucking out the scarf a little behind. 'I could do it myself, but I don't think I can explain it.'   (ch. 2)

Gertrude is here trying to connect herself with Eugenia's world of silk shawls (a world that she is just about to come into contact with). To her, though, the India scarf means not concealment but style, doing something elegantly simply for the sake of elegance itself. This is a concept she has had to invent for herself, it is instinctive and hard to explain. Charlotte, true to the tenets of New England, gently but inexorably puts her down. 'By a movement of her elbows' she corrects 'the laxity that had come from her companion's touch', and says earnestly, 'I don't think one should ever try to look pretty.' The gesture and the words reveal a way of life, but the conscious moral pressure which Charlotte is putting on her sister in this scene takes a different form, and the conversation about the India scarf is merely a tactful interlude from it. Charlotte is concerned about the sabbath-breaking which seems so innocent to James. To her it is a symptom of 'restlessness', a condition to be treated like an illness: 'I hope you will be better when we come back.' It is the effects of an upbringing full of this kind of gentle but persistent 'understanding' that have given Gertrude those eyes 'at once dull and restless'. The Wentworths have a plan for curing Gertrude of her 'peculiarities' which has much in common with Felix's plan for curing Clifford of his. Just as Felix believes that 'the more charming a woman is the more numerous, literally, are her definite social uses', so the Wentworths have an analogous belief in the moral uses of a virtuous man. Mr Brand, Gertrude's suitor, is a Unitarian minister. He is an earnest, pleasant, humourless young man, 'handsome, but rather too stout', and to Gertrude he stands for everything that she finds most oppressive in her life. For some time now she has been trying to fend off his attentions with teasing and wayward remarks, as now when she tells him that she is not going to church 'because the sky is so blue'. His baffled persistence makes it a weak defence, but unexpected reinforcements are on the way.

The family set off to church and Gertrude is left alone in the empty house:

The front door of the big, unguarded home stood open, with the trustfulness of the golden age; or what is more to the purpose, with that of New England's silvery prime. Gertrude slowly passed through it, and went from one of the empty rooms to the other – large, clear-coloured rooms, with white wainscots, ornamented with thin-legged mahogany furniture, and, on the walls, with old-fashioned engravings, chiefly of scriptural subjects, hung very high.   (ch. 2)

It is a house swept and garnished and Felix enters in, bringing the incalculable future with him. At the moment when Gertrude first sets eyes on him, he appears to be the creature of her own wish-fulfilment dream. She has been reading the *Arabian Nights* and, looking up from the page, she beheld, as it seemed to her, the Prince Camaralzaman standing before her. A beautiful young man was making her a very low bow – a magnificent bow, such as she had never seen before. He appeared to have dropped from the clouds; he was wonderfully handsome; he smiled – smiled as if he were smiling on purpose.   (ch. 2)

Felix, the adventurer, has struck it lucky. To this impressionable girl, the shoddy tale of Eugenia's marriage is the genuine stuff of romance and her husband's ridiculous title, which alerts the reader to the pettiness of the prince's status in a society where titles are ten a penny, sets the hallmark on that romance. For Gertrude, Prince Camaralzaman and the Prince of Silberstadt-Schreckenstein belong in the same box, a box of delights which she is now seeing opened for the first time in her life.

Throughout the novel Gertrude continues to see Felix as a fairy-tale prince who arrives as if he has 'dropped from the clouds' and will go away 'some day – when the leaves begin to fall', and he continues to play up to her image of him as he singles her out in a leisurely way from her sister and Lizzie Acton as the object of his lighthearted love. I suggested earlier that *The Europeans* owes something to Jane Austen, but she certainly takes a more acerbic view of plausible young men who amuse themselves by playing flirtation games with intense young women. If Felix is not a Willoughby or a Henry Crawford, so too his careless, smiling charm is untouched by any shadow of what it is to become in spineless Sir Claude and treacherous, manipulated Merton Densher. Instead he seems to come from a world which predates the novel genre and its moral concerns, the world of early Shakespearian comedy in which pairs of lovers can be juggled with and rearranged, as Felix pairs off Charlotte and Mr Brand, to achieve the final harmony of the happy ending. The last words of the novel confirm this reading, as Gertrude disappears into a distant echo of gaiety, never to be disillusioned by Felix's lightweightness or damaged by his frivolity.

What saves Felix, and with him the novel, from triviality is his vision of America. It is a vision which reminds us of another post-lapsarian Eden, the garden of Marvell's 'Upon Appleton

House', but where Marvell sees his garden in the context of a chaotic because fallen world, Felix, untouched by the sombreness of the puritan tradition, sees what is truly a New World in which nature is both ordered and free. To Eugenia it is a land of barbarians, to Gertrude it is a prison for the spirit, to the rest of the Wentworth circle it is simply the place where they live, but Felix sees it like a pastoral painting, bathed in crystalline air and light. This picture of an almost sinless paradise is endorsed by James himself, and the clarity with which he draws it gives the book its charm:

The day was the perfection of summer weather; the little lake was the colour of sunshine; the plash of the oars was the only sound, and they found themselves listening to it. They disembarked, and, by a winding path, ascended the pine-crested mound which overlooked the water, whose white expanse glittered between the trees. The place was delightfully cool, and had the added charm that – in the softly-sounding pine-boughs – you seemed to hear the coolness as well as feel it. Felix and Gertrude sat down on the rust-coloured carpet of pine needles and talked of many things.   (ch. 7)

Nevertheless it is Gertrude, only partly realized though she is, who remains James's most interesting creation. In a novel which resolutely turns its back on pain, she is the character with the greatest capacity for feeling, and before she can escape into the longed-for sphere of gaiety she has first to release and then cauterize that feeling in a scene which strikes an unexpected chill in the reader. Gertrude has finally rejected Mr Brand, and with him the values he so consciously stands for. Though his declaration of love seems 'flat and mechanical' to her, to us his sincerity is evident and moving:

He looked at her again; and then, very gently, 'No I will not avoid you,' he replied; 'but I will leave you, for the present, to yourself. I think you will remember – after a while – some of the things you have forgotten. I think you will come back to me; I have great faith in that.'

This time his voice was very touching; there was a strong, reproachful force in what he said, and Gertrude could answer nothing. He turned away and stood there, leaning his elbows on the gate and looking at the beautiful sunset. Gertrude left him and took her way home again; but when she reached the middle of the next field she suddenly burst into tears. Her tears seemed to her to have been a long time gathering, and for some moments it was a kind of glee to shed them. But they presently passed away. There was something a little hard about Gertrude; and she never wept again.

(ch. 5)

It would not be an exaggeration to say that this paragraph is unlike anything else in the novel. In its cold if glancing acknowledgement that Felix's sunny programme for his future with Gertrude must be paid for by someone, and the psychological truthfulness of its account of how that price is paid, it points us forward to James's major work.

The cauterization of feeling is a central theme in the next novel I want to look at, *Washington Square*. This book is a small-scale masterpiece, a study of controlled sadism, written with a mocking elegance that almost persuades us that James is amused by what he shows us. It is a story as cruel, though not as complex, as any James was ever to tell. There are only three essential characters, the young heiress Catherine Sloper, her father and her handsome and plausible suitor, though all the way through the novel a fourth character, Catherine's foolish widowed aunt Mrs Penniman, tries to steal a slice of the action in a drama which is no business of hers and which she fails to understand. The plot of the novel is very simple. Catherine is the only child of her father, a rich and successful doctor. She is courted by a charming, penniless young man who is at once assumed by Dr Sloper to be a fortune-hunter, largely on the spurious grounds that Catherine is so stupid and unattractive that her suitor must have an ulterior motive. His premises are faulty, but, as we gradually realize, his conclusion is correct; Morris Townsend is indeed a fortune-hunter. The girl, torn between erotic and filial love, tries to win her father over and demonstrate her lover's good faith by a gentle, patient capacity to wait. In the end, the father takes his daughter to Europe for a six-month tour, which in fact he extends to a year, and at the end of this lengthy separation Catherine, returning to America aware that she will never gain her father's consent and ready at last to marry her lover without it, is cruelly jilted by Townsend in a way that appears to confirm completely her father's reading of the whole affair. (We shall look later at the ingenious final twist which makes the novel, unlike its basic plot material, not simple at all.)

Curiously enough, James takes much of the material of *Washington Square* from a very different novel, Jane Austen's sparkling *tour de force, Northanger Abbey*. It was there that he found the idea of a heroine whose 'ordinariness' appears to exclude her from the genre she inhabits – it is no accident that James's heroine too is a Catherine – and of the cold paternal tyranny which can operate unchecked within the civilized confines of daily life. However, while much of the comedy in Austen's novel springs from its heroine's naïve attempts to read 'real life' in terms of sensational fiction, in James's novel this function is displaced on to Catherine's aunt:

> Mrs Penniman's real hope was that the girl would make a secret marriage, at which she should officiate as brideswoman or duenna. She had a vision of this ceremony being performed in some subterranean chapel – subterranean chapels in New York were not frequent, but Mrs Penniman's imagination was not chilled by trifles – and of the guilty couple – she liked to think of poor Catherine and her suitor as the guilty couple – being shuffled away in a fast-whirling vehicle to some obscure lodging in the suburbs, where she would pay them (in a thick veil) clandestine visits, where they would endure a period of romantic privation, and where ultimately, after she should have been their earthly providence, their intercessor, their advocate, and their medium of communication with the world, they should be reconciled to her brother in an artistic tableau, in which she herself should be somehow the central figure.   (ch. 15)

It is against such fake romantic scenarios as this that we are enabled to measure the force of Catherine's unswerving unselfdramatizing integrity, which her aunt, of course, takes for insensibility.

Mrs Penniman is a Restoration-comedy figure, a sort of great-niece of Sheridan's Mrs Malaprop, and her trivializing presence contributes to the curiously detached tone of the narrative. However, she is not alone in distorting Catherine's story to suit the requirements of her own imagination. Dr Sloper, in his attempt to extract some kind of damaging admission from Townsend's sister, gives his own special-pleading account of it.

'I am sure that if you were to see Catherine, she would interest you very much. I don't mean because she is interesting in the usual sense of the word, but because you would feel sorry for her. She is so soft, so simple-minded, she would be such an easy victim! A bad husband would have remarkable facilities for making her miserable; for she would have neither the intelligence nor the resolution to get the better of him, and yet she would have an exaggerated power of suffering. I see,' added the doctor, with his most insinuating, his most professional laugh, 'you are already interested!' (ch. 14)

Throughout the novel Dr Sloper holds obstinately to the theory of his daughter's feeblemindedness, even as he vainly attempts to break her will. This enterprise, which he at first sees as offering 'a prospect of entertainment', in fact has its origins in the hidden, irrational springs of a mind which likes to see itself as wholly scientific. It becomes an obsession, and in pursuit of it he unleashes on Catherine all the arts of the emotional blackmailer, a simulated gamut that runs from tenderness to bitter reproach. His tactics are almost those of a seducer, and confronted by *his* 'remarkable facilities for making her miserable' Catherine has no means of defending herself:

She lay staring at the uncomforting gloom, with her eyes and ears filled with the movement with which her father had turned her out of his room, and of the words in which he had told her that she was a heartless daughter. Her heart was breaking. She had heart enough for that. At moments it seemed to her that she believed him, and that to do what she was doing, a girl must indeed be bad. She *was* bad; but she couldn't help it. (ch. 19)

Catherine suffers, but she is not 'an easy victim', defended as she is by an inner strength that she never fully recognizes in herself. It is a strength that we are first introduced to at the start of the novel when James gives us a moral description of his heroine which parallels Austen's similar description of Catherine Morland. Of Austen's Catherine we learn that

her heart was affectionate, her disposition cheerful and open, without conceit or affectation of any kind – her manners just removed from the awkwardness and shyness of a girl; her person pleasing, and, when in good looks, pretty – and her mind about as ignorant and uninformed as the female mind at seventeen usually is.   (ch. 2)

James's description has an important element that Austen's lacks:

She was excellently, imperturbably good; affectionate, docile, obedient, and much addicted to speaking the truth.   (ch. 2)

As the novel progresses, this goodness, which initially appears passive and unwilled, develops into an enduring capacity for love and faithfulness, and later, when that love has been rewarded by a double betrayal, into a capacity simply to endure. This is all that is left to her, for though her father fails to the end to break her will, he finally succeeds in breaking something else:

From her own point of view the great facts of her career were that Morris Townsend had trifled with her affection, and that her father had broken its spring. Nothing could ever alter these facts; they were always there, like her name, her age, her plain face. Nothing could ever undo the wrong or cure the pain that Morris had inflicted on her, and nothing could ever make her feel towards her father as she felt in her younger years. There was something dead in her life, and her duty was to try and fill the void.   (ch. 32)

Unselfdramatizing as ever, she goes 'with an even and noiseless step, about the rigid business of her life', and the clever young lawyer who finally disproves the doctor's theory that 'no young man, with a moustache or without, will ever be in love with Catherine' finds that his solicitations fall on deaf ears.

   It is at this point, where a more straightforward novelist would have brought Catherine's story to an end, that James's novel becomes really interesting. Dr Sloper has seen Morris Townsend vanish out of Catherine's life without tasting the 'little triumph that he had rather counted on', the triumph of underlining his daughter's pain by forcing her to admit to having been jilted. All through the long years of Catherine's uneventful spinsterhood, this defeat has rankled, and because of it his obsession with Townsend has never left him. Though 'obliged to recognize the fact that if the two young people were waiting for him to get out of the way, they were at least waiting very patiently', he is unable to shake off the idea that Townsend is still lurking somewhere, concealed but malevolent. Finally, after half a lifetime in which Catherine has never heard him mention Townsend's name, he puts this obsessive thought into words: 'Promise me not to marry Morris Townsend after I am gone', and Catherine, 'affectionate, docile, obedient' Catherine, at last says no.

In the very simple words of the conversation that follows James charts the gulf of incomprehension between father and daughter. Catherine has no way of explaining that her refusal is not due to any lingering concern with Morris Townsend but is a defence of the human dignity that her father had injured when she was young and is insulting now. He, failing to understand this, believes that her defiance is proof of her continuing interest in Townsend, and when he dies a year later she finds that he has taken a posthumous revenge on her. He has changed his will, and the bulk of the money, that money for the sake of which Townsend had courted and jilted her, the money her father had been so eager to protect, is to go to an assortment of hospitals and medical schools. Catherine neither needs nor wants the money, but again her father has managed to add new insult to old injury. The codicil which disinherits her speaks, with now unanswerable contempt, of her fondness for 'unscrupulous adventurers'. But Catherine has the measure of her father now, and the dead man fails after all to have the last word. When the outraged Mrs Penniman says, 'Of course you will dispute the will', she replies gently, without irony, 'I like it very much. Only I wish it had been expressed a little differently!'

The novel still has one more twist. Once again, though her father's premises were faulty his conclusion was correct; after his death Morris Townsend comes back into Catherine's life. Encouraged by the incorrigible Mrs Penniman, his avidity shrunk by middle age, he has returned in pursuit of the scraps of Catherine's fortune. To say no to her father was a moral victory for Catherine; to say no to Morris Townsend is not even to banish a ghost of the past:

It seemed to be he, and yet not he; it was the man who had been everything, and yet this person was nothing. How long ago it was – how old she had grown – how much she had lived! She had lived on something that was connected with *him*, and she had consumed it in doing so.   (ch. 35)

Looking at this person who is nothing, looking into and through him, she recognizes the pattern of his life: 'he had made himself comfortable, and he had never been caught'. With the authority that this recognition confers on her, she dismisses him from her house. The novel ends, in a refinement of authorial cruelty, with Townsend reproaching Mrs Penniman in the hall while Catherine, in the parlour, picks up 'her morsel of fancywork' and sits down with it again '– for life, as it were'.

Washington Square makes explicit the possibilities of betrayal that *The Europeans* evaded, but it does so with a dry and distanced elegance that is disturbing rather than moving, disturbing because, as the final sentence shows, the wit of the narrative, its mocking *Northanger Abbey* tone, seems to range the author himself on the side of Catherine's oppressors. Catherine's plight is exemplary and is displayed to us with a brilliant economy of means, but when put alongside James's later work the novel is like words that have not yet been set to music. James has found his major poetic theme but he has not yet learnt to make that theme poetic. It is in his next novel, *The Portrait of a Lady*, that he achieves this for the first time on the grand scale. However, the germ of *Portrait* had already been sown before James wrote *The Europeans*, in a short story which established him as a notable writer. That story is *Daisy Miller*.

Daisy, like Isabel Archer, is a young American girl experiencing the delights and the hidden dangers of Europe for the first time. Unlike Isabel, however, she is an uncultured little provincial flirt with a rich father back home in Schenectady and a circle of gentleman admirers. We are informed early in the story by her appalling little brother that 'her real name is Annie P. Miller'. Much of the odd poetry that underlies the tale comes from James's use of the associations evoked by the name Daisy. It is not her real name, but it seems to evoke her real nature. She has a 'bright, sweet, superficial little visage'. She is described as 'very common' and 'completely un-cultivated'. At the end of the story, when what had seemed to be sparkling social comedy has culminated in the sudden and terrible death of the heroine, we see the 'raw protuberance' of her grave 'among the April daisies'.

This daisy imagery is connected with the teasing idea of Daisy's innocence which so preoccupies Winterbourne, the dilettante intellectual through whose eyes we see the events of the story. The problem is partly a cultural one – Daisy's flirtation games, which would have been taken at face value back home in Schenectady, seem to the Europeanized Americans of Vevey and Rome to be 'appearances' which signal even worse excesses. The very frankness of Daisy's behaviour counts against her:

Would a nice girl – even allowing for her being a little American flirt – make a rendezvous with a presumably low-lived foreigner? The rendezvous in this case, indeed, had been in broad daylight, and in the most crowded corner of Rome; but was it not impossible to regard the choice of these circumstances as a proof of extreme cynicism?
(ch. 3)

The cultural divide here is created by class as well as geography. By the standards of Winterbourne's circle, Daisy is vulgar and the fact that she is also richer than they are only makes matters worse. However, Daisy has spotted a genuine ethical difference between Europe and America when she says of flirtation, 'It seems to me much more proper in young unmarried women than in old married ones.' Daisy's 'inno-cence', on this level, means both her ignorance of social codes and her sexual intactness. It is the second of these that really preoccupies Winterbourne. However, if we think of Daisy as personifying the flower she is named after, we see her innocence in a new light. The end of the story says, 'How small a part of time they share, / That are so wondrous sweet and fair', while reminding us at the same time that after all she was only a pretty little weed. Neither Giovanelli, who has led her to her death, nor Winterbourne, whose inability to take seriously his own sexual attraction to her has lost him the chance of rescuing her from her fate, is capable of really mourning for Daisy.

Daisy Miller contains the germ of *The Portrait of a Lady*, but for the novel to come into being James also needed the powerful influence of George Eliot's *Daniel Deronda*. How this operated we shall see in the next chapter.

CHAPTER 3

The Portrait of a Lady

F. R. Leavis in *The Great Tradition* reprints James's 'Daniel Deronda: A Conversation', a perceptive and witty critical piece in which three different readers discuss George Eliot's novel, expressing three different opinions of it, all of them valid. Theodora, who is modelled on, and named after, the Dorothea of *Middlemarch*, takes the high-mindedly approving line that Dorothea herself might have taken if she had had the opportunity to read Eliot's novel; Pulcheria, frivolous but sharp-minded, focuses on the book's defects; while Constantius takes a judicial middle view, which James is careful to prevent the reader from assuming too easily to be his own. Leavis advances the 'Conversation' as proof of the influence of Eliot's Gwendolen Harleth on James's Isabel Archer, drawing particular attention to Theodora's description of Gwendolen as

a perfect picture of youthfulness – its eagerness, its presumption, its preoccupation with itself, its vanity and silliness, its sense of its own absoluteness. But she is extremely intelligent and clever, and therefore tragedy *can* have a hold on her

which he tricks the reader into taking for a moment to be a description of 'some girl encountered in actual life' whom James had in mind when creating Isabel. I think that Leavis was undoubtedly right about the influence of Gwendolen on Isabel, but that influence operated in a more subtle way than his analysis of her as 'Gwendolen Harleth seen by a man' would suggest. The key to this is another passage from the 'Conversation':

CONSTANTIUS: Think now a little about poor Gwendolen.

35

PULCHERIA: I don't care to think about her. She was a second-rate English girl who got into a flutter about a lord.
THEODORA: I don't see that she is worse than if she were a first-rate American girl who should get into exactly the same flutter.
PULCHERIA: It wouldn't be the same flutter at all; it wouldn't be any flutter. She wouldn't be afraid of the lord, though she might be amused at him.

The point is, after all, a simple one: the influence of one great artist on another does not result in imitation but rather in the creative reworking of a problem, which in this case, as Pulcheria's retort suggests, is one of plot as well as of character. When James, in the preface to *Portrait* in the New York edition, claimed that, looking back, he perceived that the germ of his idea 'must have consisted not at all in any conceit of a "plot"' but rather in 'the conception of a certain young woman affronting her destiny' he is in a sense being disingenuous. Leavis is almost certainly right that, in finding his imagination possessed by the image of Isabel, James was thinking of 'some girl encountered in actual life'. (It was not until twenty years later, when he wrote *The Wings of the Dove*, that James was able to set down what that girl's destiny had been.) But though it was Isabel herself who formed the original inspiration for the novel, and probably the strength of her imagined presence which enabled James to transcend the limitations of his previous fiction, the formula with which he describes his first conception of her makes it plain that her character could only be expressed through her predicament. She is 'affronting her destiny', and that destiny is closely related to Gwendolen's.

Let us look, to begin with, at a few biographical facts. Gwendolen Harleth has been brought up by a timid and doting mother, her father having died when she was a baby. Her relationship with this mother is bullying and demanding, but is at bottom one of deep emotional dependence. She has four younger half-sisters, all of whom look up to her as a superior being and are despised by her in return as stupid and commonplace. The youngest of these sisters is called Isabel. At the start of the novel, Gwendolen's hated and mainly absentee stepfather has just died, enabling the family to return from a life of aimless continental wanderings and settle in England near Gwendolen's uncle and aunt. One consequence of this move is that her cousin Rex, a healthy and fresh-faced young man, presently falls in love with her, despite the discouragement of his father who disapproves of the attachment largely on the grounds that Rex cannot afford to support a wife. Nevertheless, Rex attempts to propose to Gwendolen and is repulsed by her with a cold indifference which is followed, once he has gone, by a fit of hysterical weeping in which she declares that she will never love anyone.

Isabel Archer, by contrast, has been brought up by her irresponsible and dissipated father, her mother having died when she was very young. Her attitude to her father has always been one of unquestioning admiration and love and she, in return, has always been his favourite daughter. She is the youngest of three sisters, and regards the middle sister Edith as far prettier than herself. At the start of the novel Isabel's father has recently died and her eccentric expatriate aunt has suddenly arrived and taken her to England to stay with her uncle, an elderly and invalid retired banker. One consequence of this visit is that Isabel's cousin Ralph, a highly intelligent young man who is slowly dying of tuberculosis, becomes emotionally and imaginatively involved with her, while she develops a sisterly affection for him. Despite the encouragement of his father, he declines to propose to Isabel, but arranges instead for his father to leave her a fortune. Isabel, meanwhile, has turned down two ardent proposals, one from an English peer and one from an American businessman, feeling a mixture of fear and elation at doing so, along with an alarmed sense that she might be 'a cold, hard, priggish person'.

It will already be clear that the difference between Isabel and Gwendolen is not simply a matter of the gender of the eye that observes her. James, in fact, is following up Pulcheria's suggestion of a story in which a first-rate American girl doesn't get into a flutter about a lord, by turning Eliot's novel, or at any rate that part of it that interests him, the part that Leavis called '*Gwendolen Harleth*', upside down. We shall see presently the effect this has on the working out of the plot. Let us look

first at the effect it has on Isabel herself. In a sense Eliot arrived
at the character of Gwendolen by taking Rosamond Vincy, the
perfect blonde wax doll whose appearance masks a relentless
and devouring egotism, and endowing her with the passionate
inner life of Dorothea Brooke. Gwendolen is Dorothea's
opposite; by making Isabel Archer, in her turn, Gwendolen's
opposite, James is engaging with *Middlemarch* as well as with
Daniel Deronda. It is noteworthy that Theodora's description of
Gwendolen will serve as well for the Dorothea of the opening
chapters of *Middlemarch* as it will for Isabel. All three girls, in
their different ways, are eager, presumptuous and self-
preoccupied. All three have the potential for tragedy.

In Gwendolen's case, an exaggerated and imperious self-
confidence is accompanied by a terrified shrinking away from
certain areas of self-knowledge. There are three key episodes
early in the novel which establish the nature of this fear. In the
first of these, Gwendolen, as a child, strangles her sister's canary
'in a final fit of exasperation at its shrill singing which had
again and again jarringly interrupted her own'. The description of Gwendolen replacing the murdered canary with a
white mouse, a pet which will stay satisfactorily silent, and
excusing herself on the grounds of her 'peculiar sensitiveness',
is comic, but the definition of the killing as 'one of those
passionate acts which look like a contradiction of habitual
tendencies' strikes a warning note. Gwendolen, although she
doesn't realize it, is potentially psychotic and this will have a
bearing on the end of the novel. It is interesting that one of
Isabel's more Dorothea-like traits is in fact an inversion of
Gwendolen's capacity for involuntary and unpremeditated
cruelty:

She had resented so strongly, after discovering them, her mere errors
of feeling (the discovery always made her tremble as if she had
escaped from a trap which might have caught her and smothered her)
that the chance of inflicting a sensible injury upon another person,
presented only as a contingency, caused her at moments to hold her
breath. That always struck her as the worst thing that could happen
to her.   (ch. 6)

In the second episode, Gwendolen, while playing charades,
is suddenly confronted by the image of 'an upturned dead face,

from which an obscure figure seemed to be fleeing with outstretched arms'. She has already seen this picture, painted on the inside of a panel which has suddenly sprung open, once before, and both times it is 'the small Isabel' who is responsible for its appearance. In the charade, which has been contrived to show her off in Greek dress, Gwendolen represents the Hermione of *The Winter's Tale*, with the unfortunate Rex as Leontes. It is made clear that Gwendolen has no understanding of the significance of the scene she is to play, in which Hermione, by revealing that she is not a statue but living flesh, wordlessly expresses her forgiveness of her husband's irrational cruelty. The cue for the unfreezing of Gwendolen is a 'thunderous chord' on the piano, played, significantly, by Herr Klesmer, who is later to explain to her so devastatingly the difference between being a drawing-room amateur and being an artist. That 'thunderous chord', the intrusion of real art into 'an imitation of acting', is also the cue for the starting open of the panel with its ghostly picture, and Gwendolen, after one piercing cry, is frozen into a statue of a different kind, 'a statue into which a soul of Fear had entered'. That dead face and the terror of it are also to recur at the end of the novel.

In *Portrait*, the small Isabel's curiosity about the painted panel is transformed into the scene in which Isabel insists on being shown the pictures in the Gardencourt gallery, and then asks Ralph whether the house has a ghost. When he tells her that the ghost can only be seen by those who have suffered, and adds, 'I saw it long ago', she tells him presumptuously that she is not afraid.

> 'You're not afraid of suffering?'
> 'Yes, I'm afraid of suffering. But I'm not afraid of ghosts. And I think people suffer too easily ... It's not absolutely necessary to suffer; we were not made for that.'   (ch. 5)

When Ralph, whose glancing reference to his own mortal illness she has failed to pick up, agrees that she at least is not, she adds with a certain bitterness, 'Only, if you don't suffer they call you hard.'

The third of the key episodes in *Daniel Deronda* has been mentioned already, Gwendolen's fit of hysterical weeping, after

Rex's declaration of love, in which she clings to her mother and tells her, 'I can't bear anyone to be very near me but you.' This has a crucial importance not only for Gwendolen's story but also for Isabel's. Eliot published her novels at a period when an explicit account of the sexuality of her characters would have been unacceptable to the reading public, but in the cases of both Dorothea and Gwendolen she managed to evade this prohibition, accurately portraying their sexual natures through indirect and often symbolic means. In Dorothea's case the uneasy lack of self-awareness of a passionate girl, ignorant about her own sexual drive which she attempts to sublimate into moral fervour, is brilliantly captured in the episode in which she is stirred into contradictory behaviour and conflicting emotions by the beauty of the jewels left to her by her mother. It is this ignorance about her own sexuality which allows her to marry the dried-up Casaubon, whose own 'stream of feeling' is so shallow that it can afford him no more than a ritual sprinkling. James was fully aware of this aspect of Eliot's novel; in the 'Conversation' he makes Constantius say, 'If Dorothea had married any one after her misadventure with Casaubon, she would have married a trooper.' In *Daniel Deronda*, Eliot gives us the opposite case. What Gwendolen is struggling to conceal from herself is not sexual desire but pathological sexual revulsion. Hence the distress with which she responds to her own rejection of the harmless and amiable Rex, and hence too, fatally, her willingness to contemplate marriage with the reptilian Grandcourt, an accomplished sadist whose drawling impassivity she mistakes for indifference.

All this has an important bearing on *Portrait*. Isabel has Gwendolen's terror of sex, but the high-mindedness she shares with Dorothea, the tendency to see life in moral terms, often simplifying and consoling ones, enables her to bury her fear deeper than Gwendolen can do. In marrying Gilbert Osmond she is on one level acting like Dorothea, moved by a naïvely noble ideal of service to a greatness that she alone can perceive and as deceived by Osmond's sterile aestheticism as Dorothea is by Casaubon's impotent scholarship. On another and a deeper level she is acting like Gwendolen, choosing a man far older than herself who appears to make a virtue of restraint and failing to see the egotism behind the mask of self-effacing austerity.

If all three girls marry in a state of ignorance about their own sexual natures and those of their prospective husbands, the disasters of their married lives are given an added significance for us, and for the onlookers inside the individual novels, by another characteristic which they share. Each of them appears, to herself and to others, to be a 'remarkable' person. In Dorothea's case this specialness is felt to be a moral one. She is a latter-day Saint Theresa without a cause, and if she appears more intellectual than her friends and acquaintances this is a matter of intensity rather than scholarship. When compared with Mary Garth's sharp and disciplined intelligence, Dorothea's ardent yearnings appear unfocused and absurd, yet Eliot allows her moral arrogance and intransigence to be transformed by suffering into a kind of secular sainthood. In Gwendolen's case she has no such illusions. Gwendolen's remarkableness exists mainly in the minds of the family she dominates. It does have an objective correlative in

her beauty, a certain unusualness about her, a decision of will which made itself felt in her graceful movements and clear unhesitating tones, so that if she came into the room on a rainy day when everybody else was flaccid and the use of things in general was not apparent to them, there seemed to be a sudden, sufficient reason for keeping up the forms of life; and even the waiters at hotels showed the more alacrity in doing away with crumbs and creases and dregs with struggling flies in them   (Bk 1 ch. 4)

but Eliot warns us that this is a superficial explanation. Gwendolen really owes her domestic pre-eminence to a form of selfishness which her novelist has often observed in quite unattractive people, most of them male, who combined 'a strong determination to have what was pleasant, with a total fearlessness in making themselves disagreeable or dangerous when they did not get it'. However, there is more to it than this. Gwendolen is the dupe, as Dorothea is the victim, of society's readiness to compensate upper- and middle-class young ladies for their exclusion from the real power and the real work of the world by praising them lavishly, not for what they can do, but simply for being what they are. Gwendolen is accustomed to

being described as brilliant and remarkable simply on the
strength of her personality, an admiration which is revealed as
completely hollow when she thinks of turning her brilliance to
account by going on the stage.

Isabel, in her turn, shares with Dorothea an inflated
reputation for intellect and originality. She is spoken of as 'a
prodigy of learning, a creature reported to have read the classic
authors – in translations'. (Among the revisions to *Portrait* in
the New York edition, James added the information that
Isabel's cultural tastes included 'the music of Gounod, the
poetry of Browning, the prose of George Eliot', making her a
Dorothea/Gwendolen who has read *Middlemarch* and *Daniel
Deronda*.) However, like Gwendolen, she also attracts attention
through the vividness and confidence of her personal presence.
This presence is, of course, in Isabel's case as in Gwendolen's,
largely perceived as a sexual one, and its admirers are male. In
both girls, as also in Daisy Miller, who has, in J. I. M. Stewart's
phrase, 'a passion for dating and an imperviousness to the
remotest suggestion of petting', the combination of an
appearance of considerable freedom with a strong underlying
reluctance creates an effect which, in a striking and beautiful
girl, or even in a pretty one, is teasing and compelling. When
F. R. Leavis says of Daisy, 'She is utterly uneducated, and no
intelligent man could stand her for long since there could be no
possible exchange of speech with her', he is speaking with the
logic of that Houyhnhnmland of which intelligent men like to
think that they are natives. George Eliot, in the union of
Lydgate and Rosamond, shows with merciless clarity what
deficiencies it is possible for an intelligent man to overlook in a
pretty girl, particularly if he belongs to a society which rates
prettiness as a woman's highest attribute. Isabel is, of course, a
woman that an intelligent man can enjoy conversing with, but
James takes pains to make not only his male characters but also
his readers feel the force of her vibrant and emotional presence.
He takes pains, too, to remind us how much of this presence is
due simply to her youth. This youthfulness of Isabel, with all
youth's sense of its own potential and its blindness to the
possibility of failure, constitutes an important part of the pathos
of the book's development.

In considering the working out of Isabel's destiny we have to look again at *Daniel Deronda*. Gwendolen's family is suddenly plunged into poverty and, once her dream of a stage career has been shattered, her only escape from the intolerable subjection of earning her living as a governess is marriage to the wealthy and impassive Grandcourt. There is a compelling reason why Gwendolen should reject this escape route; Grandcourt has a mistress of many years' standing by whom he has several children, and Gwendolen has given this woman a promise not to interfere with her plan, a hopeless one in fact, to induce Grandcourt to marry her and make her son his heir. The dread of poverty causes Gwendolen to break this promise and to imagine that she can safely bury the memory of it, but her acceptance of Grandcourt is not wholly willed. Grandcourt is reptilian, and like a snake he hypnotizes his victim into acquiescence.

Gwendolen is quite aware that she is marrying out of expedience, but her belief that her marriage will enable her ' to mount the chariot and drive the plunging horses herself' is to prove a bitter illusion. Grandcourt discovers her broken promise to Lydia Glasher and proceeds, with the help of her own feelings of guilt, to tighten a noose of terror round her neck. In this predicament her only resource is the friendship of Deronda, the Messiah figure of the book, who, in the intervals of discovering his mission to found a national homeland for the Jews, gives her high-toned moral advice. Finally Grandcourt forces Gwendolen to go out with him in a small boat, knowing that the enforced proximity to him will be a torture to her. Gwendolen is by this time possessed by a compulsive desire to kill him, and when he suddenly falls overboard and drowns she is left not knowing whether she has helped to cause a death that she has so strongly willed, and haunted by the image of her husband's dead face. The psychological accuracy of this conclusion is somewhat diluted by Deronda's, and indeed Eliot's, belief that Gwendolen's remorse is ' the precious sign of a recoverable nature' and that she will eventually be purged by her sufferings.

James's radical reworking of this material reveals not merely the fascination of finding a different set of solutions to the problems posed by Eliot's novel, but a fundamentally different vision of life. On the one hand he frees Isabel from the constraints, both of character and of circumstance, that narrowed Gwendolen's range of choices. Isabel is given the riches that Gwendolen longed for, given them unconditionally and out of love; she is given the altruism and breadth of imagination that Gwendolen lacked; she is given a choice of eligible suitors. On the other hand he rejects Eliot's moral universe in which ethical decisions are taken, on the whole, by people with the facts in front of them, even though they may wilfully choose to blind themselves to some or all of the evidence. In the world of James's major novels the powers of destruction can work unseen, insidious and fatal as the fever that destroys Daisy Miller. The illicit union of *Portrait*, one of the crucial factors in Isabel's fate, is kept secret from her, and to some extent from the reader, until her choice has been irrevocably made. Where Lydia Glasher tried to prevent Gwendolen from marrying Grandcourt in order to gain an inheritance for her own child, the urbane and subtle Madame Merle promotes Isabel's marriage to Gilbert Osmond in the hope that Isabel's money will provide a dowry for Pansy, her unacknowledged daughter by Osmond. The realization of having been controlled where she had imagined that she was acting, however rashly, with free will is to add a special bitterness to Isabel's marital unhappiness.

James's novel differs from both *Middlemarch* and *Daniel Deronda* in giving central importance to one 'young woman affronting her destiny'. For Eliot, as her titles suggest, Dorothea's story is only one aspect of a study of a small-scale but paradigmatic society, while Gwendolen's fate is less important than that of the idealistic Deronda with his partly religious, partly political mission. This is by no means to say that James's book is unpolitical or unconcerned with the workings of society; indeed one of its major themes is the interaction between ideas of personal and political liberty. At the start of the novel Isabel believes herself to be free, just as she believes herself not to be poor, because she has been encouraged to think like this by her feckless father. 'Yes, that's the way you

were brought up – as if you were to inherit a million', says Mrs
Touchett tartly at their first meeting. This unexamined belief
in her personal freedom, which she sees as something intrinsic
to her, almost as if it were a gift like perfect pitch, co-exists with
a romantic naïvety about political ideas which makes her
lightheartedly imagine herself as Marie Antoinette:

In a revolution – after it was well begun – I think I should be a high,
proud loyalist. One sympathizes more with them, and they've a
chance to behave so exquisitely. I mean so picturesquely   (ch. 8)

while at the same time puzzling over the reluctance of radical
Lord Warburton to strip himself of all his hereditary worldly
goods. Old Mr Touchett, in his quiet way the most materialistic
of men, gently reminds her in reply that she is American:

You and I, you know, we know what it is to have lived under
democratic institutions: I always thought them very comfortable, but
I was used to them from the first. And then I ain't a lord; you're a
lady, my dear, but I ain't a lord.   (ch. 8)

The point that he is obliquely making is a shrewd one. Isabel
believes herself to be free not only because she has inherited her
father's assumptions but also because of her nationality. James
is fascinated by the psychological curiosity of a society founded
on puritan restraint which at the same time nurtures in its
citizens a strong sense of free will. It is a fascination with an
illusion, if indeed it *is* an illusion, which James is unable to
share. It is that strong sensation of free will that kills Daisy
Miller. The paradox becomes more than a mere novelist's
theme when we remember that it took a bloody and protracted
Civil War (in which two of James's brothers fought and were
smashed up, one physically and the other psychologically) to
put an end to the institution of slavery in Mr Touchett's
America of 'democratic institutions'. As a child Isabel,
significantly, had reacted to the fact of the Civil War as she was
later to react to the idea of the French Revolution, seeing it as
an emotional drama devoid of political content:

While the Civil War went on she was still a very young girl; but she
passed months of this long period in a state of almost passionate
excitement, in which she felt herself at times (to her extreme

confusion) stirred almost indiscriminately by the valour of either army. (ch. 4)

The Civil War is of central importance in James's next novel, *The Bostonians*, but it has its relevance to *Portrait* too. The young Isabel, 'stirred almost indiscriminately by the valour of either army', knows nothing about slavery either imaginatively or from experience. The adult Isabel, when she meets Pansy Osmond, fails to realize that Pansy is a creature enslaved.

Isabel's European adventures really begin, as she sits alone in her dead grandmother's empty house in Albany, with the unexpected appearance of the singular Mrs Touchett. The 'little thin-lipped, bright-eyed, foreign-looking woman' who sits 'in a well-worn waterproof' talking 'with striking familiarity of the courts of Europe' is a fairy godmother to Isabel's Cinderella. Fairy-tales, with their opposition of prince and peasant, belong in feudal societies – modern democracies relegate them to the nursery – so it is not surprising to discover that Mrs Touchett's circle of American friends in Paris constitutes a kind of expatriate *ancien régime*. We are given a typical specimen in Mr Luce:

Like many of his fellow colonists Mr Luce was a high – or rather a deep – conservative, and gave no countenance to the government lately established in France. He had no faith in its duration and would assure you from year to year that its end was close at hand. 'They want to be kept down, sir, to be kept down; nothing but the strong hand – the iron heel – will do for them,' he would frequently say of the French people; and his ideal of a fine showy clever rule was that of the superseded Empire. 'Paris is much less attractive than in the days of the Emperor; *he* knew how to make a city pleasant.'

(ch. 20)

Isabel, naïve but far from stupid, sees through these bored and occupationless people easily enough and offends them by saying so:

'You all live here this way, but what does it lead to?' she was pleased to ask. 'It doesn't seem to lead to anything, and I should think you'd get very tired of it.' (ch. 20)

However, when Gilbert Osmond, whose dream is not, like Mr Luce, to count the court carriages in the Champs-Elysées but to be an emperor himself, tells her that he has chosen to do nothing with his life except purchase minor art objects since that dream could not be fulfilled, Isabel's imagination at once touches in a 'human element' which makes Osmond's arid and futile boast of 'renunciation' into something beautiful. Her mental picture of him,

> the image of a quiet, clever, sensitive, distinguished man, strolling on a moss-grown terrace above the sweet Val d'Arno and holding by the hand a little girl whose bell-like clearness gave a new grace to childhood   (ch. 26)

is all in the key of this renunciation. She fails to perceive that Osmond is telling the truth when he talks of envying the Emperor of Russia and the Sultan of Turkey, and that the 'little girl', too old at fifteen to be so little, is his only serf.

Pansy's innocence is a very different affair from Isabel's eager and unguarded youthfulness. It is an artificial creation, achieved by a kind of bonsai technique, a trimming of the roots of the spirit. The result is 'a blank page, a pure white surface, successfully kept so', a being with 'no will, no power to resist, no sense of her own importance'. James makes her fake childishness touching as well as eerie. We have the sense that, left to grow up naturally, she might have had Catherine Sloper's unassuming goodness. Osmond's attitude to her is an index of his egotism, but his incessant control of her, the relentless aestheticism with which he keeps her 'unspotted', his refusal to let her grow up, are masked from Isabel by Pansy's own 'cultivated sweetness':

> That she would always be a child was the conviction expressed by her father, who held her by the hand when she was in her sixteenth year and told her to go and play while he sat down a little with the pretty lady   (ch. 35)

and Isabel, who from her own childhood has put such a high value on personal liberty, fails to take alarm. By the time she perceives the enormity of what is being done to Pansy she is inside the trap herself.

For Isabel, unlike Gwendolen, desperate, hypnotized but with the facts in front of her, Isabel is trapped. Even as she

prides herself on her freedom, her fate is being arranged for her
behind her back by two people, a man and a woman, a friend
and an enemy. The woman is Madame Merle, the bland,
worldly enchantress who casts her spell on Isabel in the
apparent safety of Gardencourt, summoning her with music in
the silent house as old Mr Touchett lies dying. The man is
Ralph. In the game of 'who *should* she have married' that the
novel tempts us to play, Ralph would be an easy winner if
James had not taken care to disqualify him before the contest
started. He is not only the Rex but also the Deronda of *Portrait*,
a Deronda stripped of any mission and of any future:

He was a bright, free, generous spirit, he had all the illumination of
wisdom and none of its pedantry, and yet he was distressfully dying.
(ch. 33)

If it were not for his detachment he could be a tragic figure.
In fact he takes pains to make himself into a comic one, a man
braving the fates that have snatched his life's work out of his
hands by keeping those hands permanently in his pockets. This
detachment is a kind of grace, a serene and clear-sighted gazing
into the face of death. It is also the habit of mind that leads him
to express his love for Isabel not by asking her to share with him
the remnant of his life but by the gift of a fortune. He wants to
set her free, to live vicariously in the fullness of her life by
enabling her to explore, as he can never do, all the potential of
her nature. He fails to realize that under all her eagerness and
presumptuous courage she is afraid; afraid of the uncom-
promising passion of Caspar Goodwood, afraid of escaping
from that passion into the eligible embraces of Lord Warburton,
afraid of the money that is meant to set her free. She sees in
Osmond's fake asceticism an escape from the burden of that
fear, the burden of that wealth. Disabled by his illness, deprived
by it of precisely that sense of liberty so dear to Isabel, Ralph
fails to see that Isabel's future is not something he can buy and
give to her as a mocking, affectionate gift without fatally
undermining her power over her life. 'That's a risk, and it has
entered into my calculation', he replies to his father's warning
that Isabel 'may fall a victim to the fortune-hunters'. 'I think
it's appreciable, but I think it's small, and I'm prepared to take

it.' On the last day of his life he will confess to Isabel the consequence of that risk-taking, and again in financial terms, though this time the effect is of a cry of pain. 'I believe I ruined you.'

Where Dorothea and Gwendolen, whatever the social pressures on them, are ultimately responsible for their marriage decisions, Isabel, though she too decides, is ultimately the victim of her destiny. But what dooms her, enchanted, misled, betrayed as she is, is not some dark superhuman power, like the President of the Immortals who sports with Hardy's Tess, but the hairsbreadth-fine result of a delicate balance of forces. Ralph acknowledges this when he tells Lord Warburton that there is still a chance that Isabel may not marry Osmond 'if one does nothing to prevent it'. There are indeed moments when James almost allows us to hope that she might escape, as when she thinks to herself, anticipating Ralph's objections to her engagement:

You could criticize any marriage; it was the essence of a marriage to be open to criticism. How well she herself, should she only give her mind to it, might criticize this union of her own! (ch. 33)

Or, more chillingly, when Pansy gently opens the door of her childhood cupboard of nightmares:

You'll be my stepmother, but we mustn't use that word. They're always said to be cruel; but I don't think you'll ever so much as pinch or even push me. I'm not afraid at all. (ch. 35)

Isabel too feels a chill – 'what teaching she had had, it seemed to suggest – or what penalties for non-performance she dreaded!' – but fails to ask the obvious question: from whom? But even as we hold our breath with the little circle of watchers, really we know that nothing can save her from Osmond and Osmond's uses for her.

In the second half of the novel we discover what those uses are. Like Eliot's Grandcourt, who 'never did choose to kick any animal, because the act of kicking is a compromising attitude, and a gentleman's dogs should be kicked for him', Osmond controls and degrades Isabel by forcing her to act as his proxy in the business of marrying off Pansy. Osmond is to preserve his gentlemanly distance while Isabel matchmakes and schemes

and bullies on his behalf. The Cinderella–Isabel of the start of
the novel, swept off to Europe to become a princess, has
mutated into Mrs Osmond, the cruel stepmother to Pansy's
Snow White, a transformation presaged, for the reader, by
Edward Rosier's gothic fantasy about Osmond's Roman *palazzo*
as a place where

> at picturesque periods young girls had been shut up ... to keep them
> from their true loves, and then, under the threat of being thrown into
> convents, had been forced into unholy marriages   (ch. 36)

This substitute fairy-tale is, of course, Osmond's creation, and
he puts the finishing touches on it with characteristic subtlety:

> When Pansy kissed him before going to bed he returned her embrace
> with even more than his usual munificence, and Isabel wondered if he
> meant it as a hint that his daughter had been injured by the
> machinations of her stepmother.   (ch. 46)

But a third and more ancient story lies beneath the other
two, just as the anguished and terrorized Isabel lies beneath the
cold, polished, worldly surface of 'Mrs Osmond'. It is the story
of Isabel-Persephone, trapped in the underworld by her demon
husband. This underworld theme begins with an image
adapted from *Middlemarch*: Dorothea's realization, on her
Roman honeymoon,

> that the large vistas and wide fresh air which she had dreamed of
> finding in her husband's mind were replaced by ante-rooms and
> winding passages which seemed to lead nowhither   (Bk II ch. 20)

but whereas Mr Casaubon 'had not actively assisted in
creating any illusions about himself' and is himself an object of
pity, 'lost among small closets and winding stairs', Isabel's
parallel discovery has no such mitigation. It is not Osmond but
she herself who is imprisoned in the place to which he has led
her, 'the mansion of his own habitation':

> She could live it over again, the incredulous terror with which she had
> taken the measure of her dwelling. Between those four walls she had
> lived ever since; they were to surround her for the rest of her life. It
> was the house of darkness, the house of dumbness, the house of
> suffocation. Osmond's beautiful mind gave it neither light nor air;
> Osmond's beautiful mind indeed seemed to peep down from a small
> high window and mock at her.   (ch. 42)

Her married life is in fact a kind of death; she feels herself to be 'shut up with an odour of mould and decay'.

Osmond's diabolic nature is made explicit in the scene in which Madame Merle tells him, 'You've not only dried up my tears; you've dried up my soul.' Osmond's cold reply, 'Don't you known the soul is an immortal principle? How can it suffer alteration?' recalls the retort of the black angel who comes to claim the soul of Guido da Montefeltro in Dante's *Inferno*. Like Madame Merle, Guido has been a giver of *consiglio frodolente* (advice on how to deceive), and the *nero cherubino*, having pointed out to him that it is impossible simultaneously to repent a sin and to will it, mockingly adds

> *Forse*
> *tu non pensavi ch'io loico fossi!*
>
> (XXVII, 122–3)

(Perhaps you didn't realize I was a logician!) For James, as for Dante, the deliberate and malicious deception of someone who trusts the deceiver is the darkest and most terrible of crimes, and in *Inferno* too such sinners are unable to weep. Frozen into the cold pit of Hell,

> *Lo pianto stesso lì pianger non lascia*
>
> (XXXIII, 94)

(their very tears stop them from weeping there), because their eye-sockets are filled with solid ice.

Later in the same scene Osmond torments Madame Merle by picking up a fragile porcelain cup from the mantelpiece. Unable to repent despite the ruin of her worldly ambitions, she is also unable to prevent herself from saying, 'Please be very careful of that precious object', and Osmond, replacing it, tells her that it is already cracked. If we put this image of the cracked cup alongside Madame Merle's description of herself to Isabel near the start of their acquaintance, we can see that it is in fact Madame Merle's brittle, empty soul that Osmond, her black angel, is holding in his hand:

I flatter myself that I'm rather stout, but if I must tell you the truth I've been shockingly chipped and cracked. I do very well for service yet, because I've been cleverly mended; and I try to remain in the cupboard – the quiet, dusky cupboard where there's an odour of stale

spices – as much as I can. But when I've to come out and into a strong
light – then, my dear, I'm a horror!   (ch. 19)

The mocking tone of worldly exaggeration conceals the fact
that she is telling the truth. When the Countess Gemini's
revelation finally brings Madame Merle 'out and into a strong
light', what Isabel feels, not in a gothic-novel but in a Greek-
tragedy sense, is indeed horror.

The plot of *Daniel Deronda* too hinges on a revelation of true
parentage, but the stagey tale of Deronda's opera diva mother
is merely a creaking contrivance to allow Deronda to be first
ignorant and then aware of his Jewish blood. In *Portrait* the
revelation is as central to the novel as the revelation of
Oedipus's parentage is in *Oedipus Rex*, and it has the same effect
of suddenly disclosing to the protagonist the black and
bottomless chasm which has always been hidden under the
smooth appearances of things. For Isabel the revelation is so
devastating, and its implications so far-reaching, that she is
only able to grasp at fragments of it: the fact that Osmond had
been unfaithful to his first wife, 'and so very soon'; the question
of whether he has also been unfaithful to her; pity and terror
at the thought of Madame Merle's stifled and frustrated
motherhood; and finally, and dominating everything, the
knowledge of having been used, 'the dry staring fact that she
had been an applied handled hung-up tool, as senseless and
convenient as mere shaped wood and iron'.

Isabel's response, in fact, is to relate what she has been told
to her own relationships with the other characters in the
unfolded drama and to her own image of herself as a free agent.
The alert reader, however, may notice another set of
consequences, which also contain a kind of horror. The
Countess Gemini's story raises the question, 'how old is Pansy
Osmond?' We know that she was born some time after the
death of the first Mrs Osmond, and that, in order to conceal the
identity of her real mother, Osmond

had to fit on afterwards the whole rigmarole of his own wife's having
died in childbirth, and of his having, in grief and horror, banished the
little girl from his sight for as long as possible before taking her home
from nurse   (ch. 51)

and that he had also been obliged to move from Naples to Florence to further the deception. In this elaborate subterfuge lies the explanation both of Pansy's upbringing and of her powerlessness. Faced with the problem of concealing the fact that his small daughter was younger than she should be, Osmond had hit on the expedient of bringing her up to be younger even than her real age, concealing the anomaly by drawing attention to it, while Pansy herself, deceived about her true date of birth, was easily persuaded that she 'would always be a child'. Perhaps, too, the buried memories of those early years when she was put out to nurse account for Pansy's nightmares about cruel stepmothers. It is inconceivable that Osmond himself would ever have pinched or pushed his daughter – 'a gentleman's dogs should be kicked for him'. However that may be, it is clear that not only has Pansy been lied to all her life about matters crucial to her own sense of identity, but also that her obsessively regulated upbringing, later to become the focus for Osmond's monstrous egotism, originated in his desire to escape the social consequences of his own adultery. Pansy too has been 'an applied handled hung-up tool'.

By this stage in the novel the earlier story patterns are working to their end. Edward Rosier's gothic imaginings have come true and Pansy has indeed been shut up in a convent to keep her from her true love. James had used this particular story before in an early novel, *The American*, but what in that novel was little more than the anti-catholic fantasy of a naïvely puritan author has here become a subtle moral point, a refutation of Henry Tilney's apparently rational argument in *Northanger Abbey* that in modern society, that 'neighborhood of voluntary spies', it is no longer possible for a man to murder his wife. Catherine Morland, if less embarrassed by the disclosure of her fantasy that General Tilney has murdered his, might justly have retorted that any newspaper will tell us that nonetheless murders still occur. Indeed, James's reader is tempted for a moment to jump to Catherine Morland's conclusion when the Countess tells Isabel:

His wife had really died, you know, of quite another matter and in quite another place: in the Piedmontese mountains, where they had gone, one August, because her health appeared to require the air, but where she was suddenly taken worse – fatally ill　　　　　(ch. 51)

and Osmond here is able to imprison and terrify his daughter without even overstepping the limits of socially acceptable behaviour. Madame Catherine's ambiguous little statement, 'We think it's enough,' with its two possible readings: 'We think that Pansy's father is overdoing it' and 'We think that Pansy has given in,' is as chilling as it is understated. There is no melodrama here, no going beyond the facts of experience. Henry Tilney's 'voluntary spies' have become Osmond's accomplices.

The false persona of Isabel as cruel stepmother vanishes when she says goodbye to Pansy in the convent and 'they held each other a moment in a silent embrace, like two sisters'. Pansy has already initiated this moment in her response to the news of her father's engagement – 'Oh, then I shall have a beautiful sister!' This modest assertion of equality, explained away by Osmond as 'a pretty little speech', here reaches fulfilment at last, though it is the sisterhood of victims of the same oppressor that is expressed by that silent embrace. Now only one story is left, the story of Persephone's attempted return to the daylight.

James now creates an extraordinary series of images of death as Isabel searches, desperate but fated, for a way out of the underworld. On the train journey across Europe towards Ralph's deathbed she travels in her thoughts

through other countries – strange-looking, dimly lighted, pathless lands, in which there was no change of seasons, but only, as it seemed, a perpetual dreariness of winter.

Her abnormal state of mind, at once phantasmagoric and listless, makes her arrival in London seem to her like a vision of the Inferno:

The dusky, smoky, far-arching vault of the station, the strange, livid light, the dense, dark, pushing crowd, filled her with a nervous fear

(ch. 53)

while Gardencourt, when she reaches it, is a house of the dead :

> she grew nervous and scared – as scared as if the objects about her
> had begun to show for conscious things, watching her trouble with
> grotesque grimaces. The day was dark and cold; the dusk was thick
> in the corners of the wide brown rooms. The house was perfectly still
> – with a stillness that Isabel remembered; it had filled all the place for
> days before the death of her uncle.   (ch. 54)

Finally the phantasmagoria gives way to reality and she finds
herself gazing at death itself, a strangely serene vision of
infinity, through the medium of Ralph's still-living skull:

> There was a strange tranquillity in his face; it was as still as the lid
> of a box. With this he was a mere lattice of bones; when he opened
> his eyes to greet her it was as if she were looking into immeasurable
> space.   (ch. 54)

This image, literally breathtaking for one reader at least, owes
something to the description of the apparently dying Queequeg
in *Moby Dick*:

> like circles on the water, which, as they grow fainter, expand; so his
> eyes seemed rounding and rounding, like the rings of Eternity
>   (ch. 110)

but it is also, in its encapsulation of infinite space in a nutshell,
a reminder that James was, without knowing it, a contemporary and fellow countryman of Emily Dickinson.

This series of images reaches its climax, 'at the time the
darkness began vaguely to grow grey', the first intimation of
the coming dawn, when Ralph's spirit summons Isabel to
witness his dead body:

> She opened the door with a hand as gentle as if she were lifting a veil
> from the face of the dead, and saw Mrs Touchett sitting motionless
> and upright beside the couch of her son, with one of his hands in her
> own. The doctor was on the other side, with poor Ralph's further
> wrist resting in his professional fingers. The two nurses were at the
> foot between them.   (ch. 55)

The formal arrangement of the figures turns this wholly
naturalistic scene into a *pietà*, the Madonna and St John, with
Mary Madgalene and Mary the sister of Lazarus, tending the

emaciated body of Christ. James holds the effect for a moment, as Isabel gazes at the face on the pillow, 'fairer than Ralph had ever been in life', and then it is sharply broken by Mrs Touchett in the one expression of raw grief she is ever to allow herself, 'Go and thank God you've no child.'

Ralph is dead, and dying he has made clear to Isabel the difference between life and death and asserted to her the value of love. Standing at the edge of his grave she has at last left the 'dimly lighted, pathless lands' of perpetual winter for the daylight and the spring:

> The weather had changed to fair; the day, one of the last of the treacherous May-time, was warm and windless, and the air had the brightness of the hawthorn and the blackbird ... There were tears in Isabel's eyes, but they were not tears that blinded. She looked through them at the beauty of the day, the splendour of nature, the sweetness of the old English churchyard, the bowed heads of good friends. (ch. 55)

A lesser writer, or a more optimistic one, might have ended the novel at this consoling moment, but Isabel's destiny has not yet finished with her. Her marriage vows, like Persephone's eating of the six pomegranate seeds, bind her to go down again into the underworld.

Even when she holds the dying Ralph in her arms, Isabel is unable to believe that she need not return to Osmond, and this apparent masochism has puzzled some critics and caused others to invent fake happy endings in which Isabel rescues Pansy and comes to terms with her marriage. J. I. M. Stewart, impatient to cut the Gordian knot that ties her, ascribes her acquiescence to 'the transcendentalizing of the idea of good form' and regrets that this idea 'does not permit Isabel to break even a quite common old plate over Osmond's head'. This is to underrate the curiously destructive effect on the psyche of a domestic tyranny that continually traps its victim in the toils of irrational guilt, tricking her into justifying herself for offences she has not committed – and for Osmond even Isabel's unstated thoughts are crimes – a guilt made the more intense by the fact that in the marriage ceremony she has promised not only to obey but, impossibly, to love her tormentor. Perhaps the closest

analogy to Isabel's state of mind is given by the ethologist
Konrad Lorenz's description of the behaviour of the parrots
that used to be confined in small cages in fashionable drawing-
rooms by gaolers more well-meaning than Osmond:

> Uncomprehendingly, the fond owner imagines that the bird is
> bowing, when it constantly repeats the bobbing head movements
> which, in reality, are the stereotyped remnants of its desperate
> attempts to escape from its cage. Free such an unhappy prisoner, and
> it will take weeks, even months, before it really dares to fly.
>
> (*King Solomon's Ring*, ch. 6)

Isabel is out of her cage now, but some outside impetus is
needed to bring her to the decision that she will eventually have
to make.

At this point the novel loops back on itself. On her arrival at
Gardencourt, Isabel had remembered the day when she sat like
Cinderella in her grandmother's house in Albany and her Aunt
Lydia had come, a disastrous fairy godmother, to change the
course of her destiny. But for that visit, 'she might have had
another life and she might have been a woman more blest'. She
had wondered then whether in that other life she would have
married Caspar Goodwood. Now, wearing black for the death
of her cousin, she sits down on the garden bench where she had
sat at the sunny start of the novel, a girl whose white dress was
ornamented with black ribbons in the last remnant of mourning
for her father. There, while reading a letter from Caspar
Goodwood, she had been surprised by Lord Warburton, come
to make her a proposal of marriage. Now, having just said
goodbye to a Lord Warburton suitably engaged to a young
lady of his own caste, she is surprised by Caspar Goodwood,
come, with his love for her still burningly alive, to confront her
with the truth about her misery and to offer her that life she
might have had.

At the end of *Daniel Deronda* Grandcourt drowned; Isabel
finds herself drowning now. The world 'seemed to open out, all
round her, to take the form of a mighty sea, where she floated
in fathomless waters'. The terror that she shares with
Gwendolen fights with the desire to let go, to surrender herself
to a force she has never felt before, the elemental power of male

sexuality. When Goodwood kisses her, she experiences the only real contact with physical passion of her life and it decides her fate. As soon as he releases her, she runs from him through the darkness like a terrified animal:

> She had not known where to turn; but she knew now. There was a very straight path.   (ch. 55)

The straightest path of all for a creature imprisoned for too long is the path that leads back to the cage.

When James revised *Portrait* for the New York edition he made two important changes to the last chapter. He expanded the description of the kiss from the original 'like a flash of lightning' to emphasize Goodwood's physical arousal and Isabel's helpless submission to it:

> His kiss was like white lightning, a flash that spread, and spread again, and stayed; and it was extraordinarily as if, while she took it, she felt each thing in his hard manhood that had least pleased her, each aggressive fact of his face, his figure, his presence, justified of its intense identity and made one with this act of possession   (ch. 55)

and he added a brief paragraph to the end of the book. The first edition had ended with Goodwood staring at Henrietta, who has just said to him, 'Look here Mr Goodwood, just you wait!' The ambiguity of this ending leaves open the possibility of hope. In the New York edition James closes all possibilities. Again Henrietta says, 'Just you wait!' and again Goodwood looks up at her

> but only to guess, from her face, with a revulsion, that she simply meant he was young. She stood shining at him with that cheap comfort, and it added, on the spot, thirty years to his life. She walked him away with her, however, as if she had given him now the key to patience.   (ch. 55)

CHAPTER 4

The Bostonians

If James was moved to write *The Portrait of a Lady* by his vivid mental picture of a heroine looking for the plot which would reveal her destiny, his next novel, *The Bostonians*, has at its hollow centre a girl whose fate is to be a screen onto which the fantasies of others can be projected. Verena Tarrant is that very American phenomenon, a star, and like the later stars of the cinema her rôle is to compensate for the frustrations and failures of her admirers by embodying their dreams. Her real self, if she has one, is located at the point where rival dreams intersect.

The novel is built round a series of images of Verena as she appears through the eyes of sceptical or seduced beholders. It is no accident that the first of these pairs of eyes belongs to the most sceptical, because the most dispassionate, observer of all, shrewd, laconic little Doctor Prance who declares at the outset of the novel that she doesn't want anyone to tell *her* what a lady can do. Her rapid, devastating summing-up of Verena is delivered at a point when the reader, like Basil Ransom, has merely glimpsed 'the young lady with red hair – the pretty one' among Miss Birdseye's grotesque and ageing guests:

She was Miss Tarrant, the daughter of the healer; hadn't she mentioned his name? Selah Tarrant; if he wanted to send for him. Doctor Prance wasn't acquainted with her, beyond knowing that she was the mesmerist's only child, and having heard something about her having some gift – she couldn't remember which it was. Oh, if she was his child, she would be sure to have some gift – if it was only the gift of the g— well, she didn't mean to say that; but a talent for conversation. Perhaps she could die and come to life again; perhaps she would show them her gift, as no one seemed inclined to do anything. Yes, she was pretty-appearing, but there was a certain indication of anaemia, and Doctor Prance would be surprised if she didn't eat too much candy.   (ch. 6)

Doctor Prance here makes a number of important points. The curious expression 'pretty-appearing', picked up later by Miss Birdseye's 'Well, she *is* pretty-looking', contains the idea that Verena's beauty is somehow deceptive, almost spurious, while her 'gift', of which we have not yet had a sample, is dismissed as only the gift of the gab and fatally associated with her being her father's daughter.

While there is considerable room for argument about Verena's authenticity and value, there is none whatever about Selah Tarrant, charlatan and con-man. James presents him to us as a kind of seedy and repulsive vampire with

a slow, deliberate smile, which made his mouth enormous, developed two wrinkles, as long as the wings of a bat, on either side of it, and showed a set of big, even, carnivorous teeth.   (ch. 6)

As he controls and manipulates Verena in her false inspirational trance

he threw up his arms at moments, to rid himself of the wings of his long waterproof, which fell forward over his hands   (ch. 8)

a waterproof which, we later discover, he never takes off. This vampire imagery creepily conveys the incestuous quality of his public exploitation of his daughter, which Basil Ransom is so struck and disgusted by, and gives an extra significance to that indication of anaemia spotted by Doctor Prance:

She was certainly very pale, white as women are who have that shade of red hair; they look as if their blood had gone into it.   (ch. 8)

Basil Ransom too, as he eyes Verena for the first time, provides us with a cogent image of her:

she had the sweetest, most unworldly face, and yet, with it, an air of being on exhibition, of belonging to a troupe, of living in the gaslight   (ch. 8)

an image which, significantly, he shares with Olive Chancellor:

She was so strange, so different from the girls one usually met, seemed to belong to some queer gipsy-land or transcendental Bohemia. With her bright, vulgar clothes, her salient appearance, she might have been a rope-dancer or a fortune-teller.   (ch. 11)

Verena the mesmerist's daughter has been brought up in that tawdry fringe of society where religion and politics, fraud and show-business meet, a world of phony séances and dubious communes dedicated to free thought and free love, a world presided over by the spirit of Mrs Ada T. P. Foat the fraudulent medium, her father's accomplice and muse. The ultra-respectable Mrs Farrinder also belongs to this world – much of the underlying comedy of the meeting at Miss Birdseye's derives from Mrs Farrinder's chagrin as she sizes up the threat that Verena offers to her own domination of the lucrative emancipationist lecture-circuit – and Verena herself has in-gested its values with her mother's milk:

She had been nursed in darkened rooms, and suckled in the midst of manifestations ... She had sat on the knees of somnambulists, and had been passed from hand to hand by trance-speakers.   (ch. 11)

This curious, and on the face of it deeply corrupting, infancy has led to an equally curious result. Verena is at one and the same time a vampire's victim-daughter and a nice ordinary girl; consequently she perceives her bizarre upbringing as a normal and enlightened one. Such innocence seems almost more alarming than the complicity it mimics as Verena trustingly obeys her mother's advice to ingratiate herself with the wealthy Miss Chancellor, equates the 'inspiration' which she simulates to please her father with the visions of Joan of Arc and placidly accepts Olive's buying-off of the parents she so uncritically loves and respects. Verena's own self-image, at the start of the novel, when she is not projecting herself as Joan of Arc, is a girlishly simple one:

she enjoyed putting on her new hat, with its redundancy of feather, and twenty cents appeared to her a very large sum.   (ch. 10)

If she doesn't, after all, 'eat too much candy' it is only because she can't afford to. 'You are so simple – so much like a child', Olive says to her the first time they are alone together, and then, eagerly, impetuously, initiating the real subject-matter of the novel, 'Will you be my friend, my friend of friends, beyond every one, everything, forever and forever?'

The Bostonians, to put a delicate point crudely, is a novel about lesbianism masquerading as a novel about women's rights. While the book brilliantly parodies the many perverse forms that politics can take in ordinary life, the politics of gut reaction, the politics of mercenary personal ambition, the politics of muddled idealism, not one of its characters ever advances a sensible argument either in favour of female emancipation or against it. Instead, the subject provides a smokescreen behind which James can advance into territory which on the face of it would seem totally inaccessible to a puritan male nineteenth-century novelist.

E. M. Forster (E. M. Forster of all people) famously criticized James for his characters' lack of 'carnality'. 'Their clothes', he complained, 'will not take off.' Olive Chancellor's clothes certainly never take off, but it is hard to think of a more detailed and cruel analysis of the intensity and frustration of a one-sided passion. As the novel goes on, her anguish, mockingly treated at first, begins to take on a tragic dimension. This anguish culminates in the most striking of all the many images of Verena. Olive, walking, in an agony of jealousy and loss, on the beach at Marmion while Verena sails 'somewhere in the bay' alone in a small boat with Basil Ransom, is suddenly visited by a nightmare vision:

She saw the boat overturned and drifting out to sea, and (after a week of nameless horror) the body of an unknown young woman, defaced beyond recognition, but with long auburn hair and in a white dress, washed up in some far-away cove.   (ch. 39)

This metaphor has occurred already in the novel in the scene in New York where the jealous Mrs Luna comes to Olive with spiteful surmises about Verena's relationship with Basil Ransom and Olive refrains from pointing out her real motivation: 'you know you hate Verena and would be very glad if she were drowned!' Mrs Luna's jealousy at the loss of Basil Ransom to Verena is here collated with Olive's own wish 'that Verena should sink for ever beneath the horizon, so that their tremendous trouble might never be'. However, beneath the superficial symbolism of concealed jealous hatred and desire to give up the struggle lies the real meaning of the image, which Olive, with striking emotional intelligence, decodes for herself as she realizes that 'never again to see the face of the creature she had taken to her soul would be for her as the stroke of blindness'. Her subconscious mind, with Freudian accuracy, has translated the idea of never seeing the beloved's face again into the image of Verena's faceless corpse. This scene is immediately followed by Olive's return to the apparently empty house where she finds Verena sitting by herself in the dark, 'looking at her with a silent face which seemed strange, unnatural, in the dusk'. 'The stroke of blindness' and 'the silent face ... in the dusk': in the vibration set up between these images, Olive's tragedy is expressed.

Where Basil Ransom is created from a handful of props – a Southern drawl which the reader is obliged to imagine, a wide-brimmed hat, a mother and sisters existing on a 'farinaceous diet' of hot corn-cake back on the ruined plantation – Olive is a fully realized character, and James subtly manipulates our response to her, from the initial instinctive recoil as she looks out of the page at us:

the curious tint of her eyes was a living colour; when she turned it upon you, you thought vaguely of the glitter of green ice   (ch. 3)

to the final sharing of Ransom's 'vision' of her rushing on death 'without a tremor, like the heroine that she was'. To some extent she is a mocking realization of George Eliot's idea of a modern Saint Theresa – Dorothea Brooke, if she had really been the person she imagines herself to be at the beginning of *Middlemarch*, might have been very like Olive – but James's real inspiration lay closer to home in the person of Alice James, his youngest sibling and only sister, from whose tragic life he drew Olive's neurosis, her jealousy, her lesbianism. At first sight this appears a cruel and perverse use of a close, if difficult, personal relationship; but Olive, unlike Alice, is a fighter. Instead of collapsing onto the sofa in life-long depressive illness, she rushes onto the stage of the Music Hall 'like the heroine that she was'. James never allows us to discover whether, faced with that

supreme test, Olive will find her voice at last and deliver
Verena's speech, every intonation of which she knows by heart.
We are left only with the 'quick, complete, tremendous silence'
which offers her the chance to break through the constraints
which, however Basil Ransom may dispute it, did indeed stifle
the spirits of frustrated, intelligent girls like Alice.

The Bostonians is deliberately set up to tease the reader about
James's *real* opinion of female emancipation. We never get a
straight answer to this question. However, while not only James
but his central characters turn the debate about women's rights
into a code for conducting a more primitive struggle between
the sexes, there is a political subtext to the novel of which the
characters themselves never notice the significance. Its crucial
symbol is the horse-car, the crowded and uncomfortable horse-
drawn trams which thread their way through the action of the
novel. Freedom for women, we gradually discover, is the
freedom to jump on a tram. This point is established when Basil
Ransom tries to see Miss Birdseye home. It is hardly surprising
that she is more bemused than gratified by his attempt to treat
her as an 'unprotected female'. Miss Birdseye may be a
confused and ineffectual philanthropist, but throughout her
long life of selfless endeavour she has performed acts which it
has never occurred to her to think of as courageous:

She had roamed through certain parts of the South, carrying the
Bible to the slave; and more than one of her companions, in the
course of these expeditions, had been tarred and feathered. She herself,
at one season, had spent a month in a Georgian jail. She had preached
temperance in Irish circles where the doctrine was received with
missiles; she had interfered between wives and husbands mad with
drink; she had taken filthy children, picked up in the street, to her
own poor rooms, and had removed their pestilent rags and washed
their sore bodies with slippery little hands.   (ch. 20)

But in fact, even if Miss Birdseye were really the 'innocent old
dear' that Ransom takes her for, she would still be perfectly safe
on that tram. Modern transport has disposed as effectively of
Ransom's idea that women need to be chaperoned as Miss
Birdseye herself does of his notion that 'what is most agreeable
to women is to be agreeable to men' when she turns her huge

spectacles on him with the mild enquiry, 'Do you regard us, then, simply as lovely baubles?'

Among the bit-part characters in *The Bostonians* are Verena's friend Miss Catching who works in the library at Harvard and offers 'to explain to Ransom the mysteries of the catalogue' and the waitress at the hotel in Marmion who betrays her 'limited tolerance for a gentleman who could not choose quickly between fried fish, fried steak, and baked beans'. As for the competent Doctor Prance, *her* attitude to the business of being an unprotected female resembles that of the two anonymous authors of *Unprotected Females in Norway; or, The Pleasantest Way of Travelling There*, who declared firmly in 1857, 'the only use of a gentleman in travelling is to look after the luggage, and we take care to have no luggage', before going on to recommend solid plaid skirts, hobnail shoes and a fishing-rod: 'it is the greatest resource in the world ... if kept waiting for, or in want of, a meal'.

A quiet revolution, in fact, is gradually taking place. It is Miss Birdseye, again, who puts this into words as she sits peacefully dying in the garden at Marmion:

'When I look back from here, from where we've sat, I can measure the progress ... You mustn't think there's no progress because you don't see it all right off; that's what I wanted to say. It isn't till you have gone a long way that you can feel what's been done.' (ch. 38)

This is the most serious political point that the novel makes, and only Miss Birdseye is qualified to make it because she alone among the reformers has the grace of humility. 'I haven't effected very much; I have only cared and hoped.' She had carried the Bible to the slave; but what matters to her now at the end of her life is not whether *she* has helped to free the slaves but only that the slaves are now free. It may be that she has not performed a single effectual act in her life, yet as that life draws to a close James makes us feel of her political endeavours what George Eliot at the end of *Middlemarch* says of Dorothea's personal ones:

The effect of her being on those around her was incalculably diffusive: for the growing good of the world is partly dependent on unhistoric acts; and that things are not so ill with you and me as they might have been, is half owing to the number who lived faithfully a hidden life, and rest in unvisited tombs.   (Finale)

The word 'diffusive' is the key one here. When we first meet Miss Birdseye, James tells us that her face

looked as if it had been soaked, blurred, and made vague by exposure to some slow dissolvent. The long practise of philanthropy had not given accent to her features; it had rubbed out their transitions, their meanings. The waves of sympathy, of enthusiasm, had wrought upon them in the same way in which the waves of time finally modify the surface of old marble busts, gradually washing away their sharpness, their details.   (ch. 4)

Later we learn that Doctor Prance is treating her with homeopathic medicine. An essential feature of homeopathy, of course, is that its remedies are more powerful the more dilute they are; and it is a *tour de force* of the novel that the more dilute Miss Birdseye becomes, the more powerfully she works upon our sympathies. If James, at the start of the novel, is using her partly to poke fun at the high-minded notions of his own father's circle of transcendentalist Boston friends – even the spectacles which appear to cover the entire surface of her face constitute a gentle parody of Emerson's declaration that in the presence of nature 'all mean egotism vanishes. I become a transparent eye-ball' – by the end, that Boston circle is among the faces that seem to wait for her, and, perhaps without her author's knowledge, she has turned into a sibyl.

'I did want to see justice done – to us', she tells Verena. 'I haven't seen it, but you will. And Olive will.' And of course she is right. If Olive Chancellor and Verena Tarrant Ransom live into their eighties like Miss Birdseye herself, they will see much that will shake their faith in progress. Olive will see the start of the Second World War and Verena will see the end of it and the dropping of the bombs on Hiroshima and Nagasaki; but both of them will see those dying words come true. Both of them will live to have the vote and to see the position of women radically transformed. Miss Birdseye 'belonged to the Short-Skirts League, as a matter of course'. The trams, alas, are gone; but every female reader of *The Bostonians*, as she jumps, unencumbered, onto a bus, tube or train, should spare a grateful thought for Miss Birdseye. 'Blessed are the meek: for they shall inherit the earth.'

For James himself, though, the real question, as always, is not the power of the present to shape the future but the ineradicable effects of the past on the present. He too, like his characters, is concerned with the cause of emancipation, as Ezra Pound was to declare in 1918 after the novelist's death:

Human liberty, personal liberty, the rights of the individual against all sorts of intangible bondage! The passion of it, the continual passion of it in this man who, fools said, didn't 'feel'.

Everything that is charged and ambiguous about *The Bostonians*, from the special bitterness of the rivalry between Olive and Ransom to the curious tone of the narrative itself, a levity that is like skating on thin ice, is coloured by the fact that it is set in the aftermath of the Civil War. The slaves have been freed, at the price of a conflict that has torn the country apart, but no war of liberation can end the 'intangible bondage' imposed by individuals on each other.

Olive and Ransom are both survivors and victims of the war – she has lost her brothers, he his patrimony. Now, in the uneasy return to the decencies of civilized life, they fight the war over again and Verena, untouched, radiant, submissive, is the virgin America for which they struggle. Both imagine that they are fighting to liberate her, neither cares if in the conflict she too is torn apart. It is no accident that Ransom, as he waits in the Music Hall to kidnap Verena, feels

as he could imagine a young man to feel who, waiting in a public place, has made up his mind, for reasons of his own, to discharge a pistol at the king or the president.   (ch. 41)

This near-blasphemous little reference to the assassination of Abraham Lincoln reminds us that more is at stake here than the rescue of Verena from a morbid old maid by a virile young man. Ransom means not only to marry Verena but to silence her, and in the final paragraph of the novel we see him symbolically achieve this aim:

Ransom, as he went, thrust the hood of Verena's long cloak over her head, to conceal her face and her identity. It quite prevented recognition...   (ch. 42)

Deprived of the power to exercise her gift, Verena has again become faceless, an anonymous member of the crowd. Without her gift she will never be anything else.

Verena's gift is a paradoxical one; completely meretricious and utterly enchanting, at once the self-expression of a diva and the self-exposure of an exhibit in a freak show, it is at everyone's disposal: her father, Olive, the Harvard college boys, the vast audience in the Music Hall; and yet it is as natural to her as its song is to a songbird. Ransom falls in love with her because of it, bitterly envies it (her success in propagating her views heightens the frustration of his failure to propagate his) and now proposes to suppress it altogether. What becomes of a songbird when it can no longer sing? When Verena asks him that very question, Ransom gives her a jocular and evasive answer, but James himself gives us a clue to what awaits her in her new life as an ordinary, ungifted person in the tears that she weeps 'beneath her hood' as the novel comes to a close. 'It is to be feared', he says, with a feline smoothness that reminds us of the ending of *Washington Square*, 'that with the union, so far from brilliant, into which she was about to enter, these were not the last she was destined to shed.'

CHAPTER 5

What Maisie Knew

The theme which we have been tracing through James's major novels is that of innocence betrayed, but what of an innocence that is proof against betrayal? In the first of the novels to be written in James's late style, we encounter a heroine clad, like the Lady in Milton's *Comus*, in the 'complete steel' of natural virtue. Like Milton's Lady, this heroine is a little girl; at the start of her novel she is only six years old. *What Maisie Knew* is perhaps the most perfect of James's novels. It combines the lucidity and shimmer of a little French Impressionist painting with the complexity and logic of an algebraic expression. As the terms of the expression are cancelled out to give the only possible right answer, it transcends the idea of the happy ending.

In the preface to *Maisie* which he wrote for the New York edition, James relates the real-life anecdote from which the novel grew:

The accidental mention had been made to me of the manner in which the situation of some luckless child of a divorced couple was affected, under my informant's eyes, by the remarriage of one of its parents – I forget which; so that, thanks to the limited desire for its company expressed by the step-parent, the law of its little life, its being entertained in rotation by its father and its mother, wouldn't easily prevail. Whereas each of these persons had at first vindictively desired to keep it from the other, so at present the re-married relative sought rather to be rid of it – that is to leave it as much as possible, and beyond the appointed times and seasons, on the hands of the adversary; which malpractice, resented by the latter as bad faith, would of course be repaid and avenged by an equal treachery.

This unedifying little tale immediately struck James as 'the beginning of a story', and just as quickly he saw that it lacked something; 'for a proper symmetry the second parent should marry too'. 'A proper symmetry': James's rather alarming choice of adjective here is reminiscent of the encounter of another nineteenth-century master of words with another little girl:

'Seven years and six months!' Humpty Dumpty repeated thoughtfully. 'An uncomfortable sort of age. Now if you'd asked *my* advice, I'd have said "Leave off at seven" – but it's too late now.'
'I never ask advice about growing,' Alice said indignantly.
'Too proud?' the other enquired.
Alice felt even more indignant at this suggestion. 'I mean,' she said, 'that one can't help growing older.'
'*One* can't, perhaps,' said Humpty Dumpty, 'but *two* can. With proper assistance, you might have left off at seven.'   (ch. 6)

If James's ruthless logic, as he sets up the terms of his plot, reminds us of Humpty Dumpty's, his child heroine, like Carroll's, will walk safely and undaunted through what, to an older protagonist, would be a world made nightmarish by the reversal of all norms. *What Maisie Knew* is in some ways an *Alice Through the Looking Glass* for grown-ups, and like *Alice* it depends for its effects on the child's clear vision of the grotesque, passionate, quarrelsome beings who surround her.

Like *Alice* again, and as its title suggests, *What Maisie Knew* is a novel about education, but while Alice received hers in the most conservative of Victorian schoolrooms, Maisie's education is an unconventional business. Indeed, education in the formal sense is mainly conspicuous in her life by its absence. Of her two governesses, even Maisie herself can see through Mrs Wix's qualifications as an instructress, while those of the 'showier' Miss Overmore, 'who could say lots of dates straight off (letting you hold the book yourself), state the position of Malabar, play six pieces without notes and, in a sketch, put in beautifully the trees and houses and difficult parts', are just as transparent to the adult reader. As for the glittering educational opportunities which her parents and guardians are always dangling before her – the school in Brighton, the classes 'with awfully smart

children', the music lessons – these invariably turn out to be
too expensive.

However, when it comes to the education provided not by
books but by life, Maisie, as she herself reflects towards the end
of the novel, 'had not had governesses for nothing: what in the
world had she ever done but learn and learn and learn?' To
begin with this is only rote-learning. At the age of three Maisie
already 'knew as well ... that a person could be compromised
as that a person could be slapped with a hair-brush or left alone
in the dark' and by the time she is five she can gabble off this
adult word 'amid rounds of applause'. However, even when
she is big enough to have a governess, she has not yet learnt its
real meaning. When her mother says of Miss Overmore, 'I take
her because she's a lady and yet awfully poor. Rather nice
people, but there are seven sisters at home. What do people
mean?' Maisie doesn't know what people mean, and applies
herself instead to memorizing 'all the names of all the sisters'
which she is soon able to recite 'better than she could say the
multiplication table'. It is left to the reader to guess without too
much difficulty what it is that people mean and to reflect that
no young woman with a reputation to protect would take a
place with an employer like Ida Farange.

There are many other lessons of the same sort for Maisie to
master. She learns that 'the natural way for a child to have her
parents was separate and successive, like her mutton and her
pudding or her bath and her nap'. She learns to carry messages
from papa to mamma – 'He said I was to tell you, from him,
that you're a nasty horrid pig!' – and in due course to return
mamma's reply to papa. Later these moral lessons are
supplemented by economic ones:

It was somehow in the nature of plans to be expensive and in the
nature of the expensive to be impossible. To be 'involved' was of the
essence of everybody's affairs, and also at every particular moment to
be more involved than usual. (ch. 15)

Maisie doesn't know much about money – her modest idea of
an 'expensive treat' is one involving buns and ginger-beer –
but these great truths are brought home to her at various stages

of her career by dinner-times without either mutton or pudding, by her growing legs and shrinking skirts, by 'all the lessons that, in the dead schoolroom, where at times she was almost afraid to stay alone, she was bored with not having'.

If this had been all that Maisie learnt, the book would simply be the story of a deprived child. However, very early in the course both of the novel and of her young life, 'a moral revolution ... accomplished in the depths of her nature' makes her leave rote-learning behind:

> She puzzled out with imperfect signs, but with a prodigious spirit, that she had been a centre of hatred and a messenger of insult, and that everything was bad because she had been employed to make it so. Her parted lips locked themselves with the determination to be employed no longer. She would forget everything, she would repeat nothing...   (ch. 2)

From then on Maisie is a fully responsive moral being, and if on a superficial level the things that she sees are left for the reader to interpret – the pretty way Miss Overmore holds her fork 'with her little finger curled out'; Ida's lurid eye make-up and hair dye, 'handsomely accounted for by the romantic state of her affections'; the pair of Beale's shoes that Maisie particularly admires for their 'laced yellow "uppers" and patent-leather complement' – at the same time her clear eyes perceive emotional and psychological truths hidden from her elders by their own disordered passions. These passions concern both sex and money – not only their affairs but their *affaires* are 'involved' – and it is Maisie's ignorance of these two great adult motives which enables her to see so clearly the emotions they generate: love, jealousy, spite, hatred and fear.

At the end of the novel, Mrs Wix worries that Maisie is without a moral sense; the reader can only marvel at her untutored possession of such a precociously acute one. In part this is due to the formative influence of Moddle, that excellent if unpolished nanny, who gives Maisie, during her first six years, the security on which, twentieth-century psychologists assure us, a child's later stability of character depends. Moddle's last-ditch attempt to preserve for Maisie a sense of living in a world where normal values – 'from "a mother's fond love" to "a nice poached egg to your tea"' – still obtain comes to an end when honest indignation overwhelms her lip-service 'respect' for her employer as she hears him instruct her little charge in the first of many hate-messages. Maisie's 'vivid reminiscence' of this scene must play some part in her momentous decision to stop carrying such messages, but the idea of an 'inner self' which can neutralize insults by concealing them is really given to her by Miss Overmore, whose partiality for Maisie's papa, expressed only by a wordless roll of her fine eyes, makes the idea of handing on Ida's latest attempt at character-assassination seem suddenly distasteful. This partiality is, of course, anything but disinterested and yet, disconcertingly, Maisie draws from it a real moral sustenance.

As the novel goes on, Maisie's capacity to take from her deplorable elders what she needs for survival, thriving on artificial and interested love if the real, natural article is not available, has alarming effects on those elders themselves. James, in his Preface, describes her as

bringing people together who would be at least more correctly separate; keeping people separate who would be at least more correctly together; flourishing, to a degree, at the cost of many conventions and proprieties, even decencies; really keeping the torch of virtue alive in an air tending infinitely to smother it; really in short making confusion worse confounded by drawing some stray fragrance of an ideal across the scent of selfishness, by sowing on barren strands, through the mere fact of presence, the seed of the moral life.

Maisie has taught herself not to carry hate-messages, but her own need to give and receive love and her ignorance both of sex and of the sexual proprieties which her partner-swopping parents and step-parents are infringing involve her in willing complicity with the need of illicit lovers for a chaperone and a cover-story. Even if she doesn't really bring Sir Claude and Mrs Beale together – she notices at their first encounter in her presence that they speak to each other 'almost as if they must have met before' – she certainly makes it easier for their relationship to develop. There seems to be almost no end to the uses to which a pair of scheming adults can put an unassuming and good little girl.

If Maisie is made use of, at least she is not hoodwinked. Ignorant of sex, she learns early to judge the grades and degrees

of love and can contrast Mrs Wix's desperate need of the child
who is both her meal-ticket and a substitute for her dead
illegitimate daughter with Mrs Beale's lavishly expressed but
shallow affection, and both with her mother's unconcealed
dislike of her. Later, in her encounter with the Captain, she
realizes that the love adults feel for each other, that puzzlingly
short-lived and unstable emotion, can also have its peaks as
well as its all-too-familiar troughs. Compared with the
Captain's embarrassed but stalwart declaration of his feelings
for her mother, 'Mrs Wix's original account of Sir Claude's
affection seemed as empty ... as the chorus in a children's
game'. In a brilliant stroke of poetic justice, it is Maisie's
passionate attempt to safeguard that love for her mother that
infects it with the knowledge of Ida's promiscuity which will
destroy it:

'You *do* love her?'
'My dear child – !' The Captain wanted words.
'Then don't do it only for just a little.'
'A little?'
'Like all the others.'
'All the others?' – he stood staring.
She pulled away her hand. 'Do it always!'   (ch. 16)

However, though Maisie, successful little organism that she is,
manages to extract from her two governesses the nutrients that
she needs for her moral survival, it is only when Sir Claude
comes into her life that she herself consciously feels love (her
love for poor, ugly Mrs Wix is as unconscious as it is instinctive).
Indeed, young as she is, she falls in love with him at first sight:

No, nothing else that was most beautiful ever belonging to her could
kindle that particular joy – not Mrs Beale at that very moment, not
papa when he was gay, nor mamma when she was dressed, nor Lisette
when she was new.   (ch. 8)

Already over-supplied with surrogate mothers, this surrogate
father seems to her more delightful than a new doll. To her
mother, of course, he *is* a new doll. Goodness only knows
(Maisie never does) where she got the money to buy him.
Perhaps 'her paralysed uncle. This old brute, as he was called'
has died at last and left her enough for a short-lived fling. The

nature of Sir Claude's marriage to Ida is made clear to the reader in that first scene when he says, looking hard at Mrs Beale, '*You* know who one marries, I think.' Maisie herself, though puzzled that he is so much younger than mamma, only sees this youthfulness as part of his charm.

The reader continues to be given every opportunity to judge Sir Claude. Though, as Mrs Wix says, he 'has beauty and wit and grace', even if not quite as much of them as Maisie and Mrs Wix imagine, he is also both feckless and spineless. His arrival causes all the grown-ups to take sides, Mrs Wix to fall grotesquely in love and Ida to fall violently out of it. Yet, as he performs his graceful, sketchy, negligent impression of father-hood, buying Maisie 'a huge frosted cake' when she is more in need of regular meals and 'a lovely greatcoat' to hide the shabbiness of her outgrown frock when he takes her out to tea, James somehow persuades us that this odd friendship between a decadent young man about town and a serious small girl is based on something real. It is not just that he is the source of the only fun her childhood has ever known, the only one to take her to the pantomime or push her on a swing, the only adult whose teasing is meant to make her, rather than the bystanders, laugh; Maisie's shining love for him has a quality which transcends his patent failure to deserve it, and his sole saving grace is that he knows this.

Meanwhile the logic of James's 'proper symmetry' continues to regulate the highly improper on-goings of Maisie's super-fluity of parents. Beale and Ida, their second marriages having soured even faster than their first, turn to other partners, partners who, with the exception of the naïvely trusting Captain, are as unattractive as they are wealthy. Both, by this time, have lost all interest in holding on to a daughter they have come to detest for her silent refusal to gratify their spite and each in turn severs all connection with her before vanishing, unregretted, from her life. Mrs Beale and Sir Claude, their own *affaire* by this time well established, are left as the *de facto* guardians of the child, each as proxy for his or her departed spouse. Prevented as they are by the divorce laws of the time from divorcing their adulterous partners because of their own adultery with each other, Maisie forms an ambiguous bond between them, at once their only claim to respectability and the ultimate proof of their depravity.

Maisie herself, of course, with the healthy selfishness of childhood, sees this bond as offering her the hitherto undreamed of chance of a stable home with two loving parents in it. However, by this time Sir Claude, terrified by his own complete submission to the powerful and determined Mrs Beale, has whisked Maisie off to France, and Mrs Wix, also now with a claim to consider herself *in loco parentis*, having been entrusted by Ida with Maisie's moral welfare, is trying to safeguard Sir Claude's as well, her genuine concern for him sharpened by the hope of realizing her own hopeless dream of a little home in which she would be a mother to Sir Claude and he would be a father to Maisie. These rival dreams bring Maisie and Mrs Wix into conflict for the first time, a conflict that is made worse by Mrs Wix's assumption that Maisie, having heard so much unsuitable adult conversation, must understand both the nature of the divorce laws and what it means to be a kept man or woman and is therefore condoning a state of affairs that in fact she doesn't really understand. Maisie's cross and baffled question, 'Then doesn't he pay *you* too?' leads, for a few minutes, to an open breach between them, though they make it up again 'too soon for either to feel that either had kept it up'.

Sir Claude, meanwhile, on the thin pretext of needing to chaperone Susan Ash, the homesick housemaid, has gone back to England and Mrs Beale. His promised return is preceded by the arrival of Mrs Beale herself, emerging radiant and triumphant from the sea-crossing which had almost finished off Maisie and Mrs Wix and, like Sir Claude, loudly proclaiming her new-found freedom from her hated spouse. Mrs Beale has been growing in power and beauty throughout the book and now, lovelier than ever, she takes control of both Maisie and Mrs Wix with one devastatingly urbane sentence, 'Dear lady, please attend to my daughter.' If to Sir Claude she represents the terror of '*Vénus toute entière à sa proie attachée*', to Maisie she is more like the beautiful wicked stepmother of a fairy-tale in which Maisie herself suddenly seems to be playing the passive part in a case of violent substitution. A victim was what she should surely be if the issue between her step-parents had been settled by Mrs Beale's saying: 'Well, if she can live with but one of us alone, with which in the world should it be but me?' (ch. 28)

While Mrs Wix begins to succumb to Mrs Beale's blandishments, Maisie watches the process with disenchanted eyes:

What her stepmother had clearly now promised herself to wring from Mrs Wix was an assent to the great modification, the change, as smart as a juggler's trick, in the interest of which nothing so much mattered as the new convenience of Mrs Beale. (ch. 28)

The trick doesn't work for Maisie. She no longer wants two parents; now she will accept only Sir Claude, 'him alone or nobody', though when Mrs Wix cries, 'Not even *me*?' Maisie expresses her calm certainty that Mrs Wix's love for her is too secure even to need thinking about with the odd little rejoinder, 'Oh you're nobody!'

And now, at last, Maisie is woken by Mrs Wix with the news that Sir Claude has come back. In order to interpret what happens next, we need to have some idea of Maisie's age. Is she really still a little girl or, as some critics have supposed, already old enough for her feelings for Sir Claude to be becoming erotic rather than filial? In order to establish this point for certain I tried the experiment of logging Maisie through the novel. James has made sure that this is not altogether easy to do – Maisie herself at one point loses track of her 'alternations of residence' – but by noting and collating every reference to the passing of time it is possible to establish without too much doubt that Maisie, in the final scenes of the book, is about eleven and a half years old. That she is still physically a little girl is confirmed by the scene in the hotel where, putting on her hat to go out, she has to stand on tiptoe to see herself in the overmantel mirror, only to be brought down to her heels by Mrs Wix's suddenly saying: 'Haven't you really and truly *any* moral sense?'

It is Maisie's moral sense that is to be tested in the final scenes of the book; but not her moral sense alone. It is one of the brilliant strokes of the novel that James subjects her to this final test at a time when all her other senses are engaged and stimulated by her first experience of 'abroad'. Apart from the opening chapter which sets up the plot, we are given the whole action of the novel through Maisie's eyes, but up to this point what she sees – telling details of dress or behaviour which her inexperience is often unable to interpret – has been less important than the emotional truths that she perceives. Now she is suddenly overwhelmed by 'the great ecstasy of a larger impression of life'. Without a single passage of extended description, James creates, through a few bright brush-strokes, not merely a sense of place but of how that place acts on an eager and untouched consciousness:

The place and the people were all a picture together, a picture that, when they went down to the wide sands, shimmered, in a thousand tints, with the pretty organization of the *plage*, with the gaiety of spectators and bathers, with that of the language and the weather, and above all with that of our young lady's unprecedented situation. For it appeared to her that no-one since the beginning of time could have had such an adventure or, in an hour, so much experience.

(ch. 22)

The *plage*, with its 'spectators and bathers', was a favourite subject of the Impressionist painters. Indeed, Manet, in 1869, had painted not only the beach at Boulogne but also the jetty along which Maisie walks with Sir Claude and the departure of the Folkestone boat which, at the end of the novel, Maisie and Mrs Wix will catch by the skin of their teeth; while the little girl in Degas's *Beach Scene*, having her wet hair combed out by her elderly nurse while her bathing-suit dries on the sand, might almost be Maisie herself. Not quite, though; preoccupied by Sir Claude's failure to return from England, she goes with Mrs Wix to sit meditatively on the old ramparts, on 'that old bench where you see the gold Virgin', instead of 'plunging into distraction with the crowd on the sands or into the sea with the semi-nude bathers'. But, of course, James is not recalling an Impressionist painting here, Maisie is creating one through the immediacy of her quick, fresh perceptions.

In his Preface James declares that his protagonist could not possibly have been 'a rude little boy'; but Maisie's instant recognition, on landing on French soil, that 'her vocation was to see the world' echoes the experience of one particularly thoughtful little boy who was to remember all his life the excitement of gazing 'from the balcony of an hotel that hung, through the soft summer night, over the Rue de la Paix' and feeling, though he had 'but just turned twelve', that he had always been a Parisian. Maisie too, like the young Henry James, is entranced by the view from a hotel balcony:

She hung again over the rail; she felt the summer night; she dropped down into the manners of France. There was a café below the hotel, before which, with little chairs and tables, people sat on a space enclosed by plants in tubs; and the impression was enriched by the flash of the white aprons of waiters and the music of a man and a woman who, from beyond the precinct, sent up the strum of a guitar and the drawl of a song about 'amour'. Maisie knew what 'amour' meant too, and wondered if Mrs Wix did.   (ch. 26)

Maisie's one innocent vanity is her pride in 'knowing' things. By the end of the novel she will have justified this claim to know what 'amour' means.

At this point the task of the critic becomes a frustrating one. This last section of the book is at once so complex and so crystalline that ideally I would like to annotate every line as one would do with a great poem, but space does not permit. I can only compensate for, in James's words, my rough overtracing of his subtleties by saying that the prose here has the economy of great poetry, in which no detail is added for the sake of ornament alone, and that it is with the kind of intelligent attention that we have to bring to the syntax and the nuances of great poetry that it should be read. In essence, what happens is that Maisie, with a new maturity of vision, finds herself seeing the true nature of the stepfather she has hero-worshipped:

She seemed to see at present, to touch across the table, as if by laying her hand on it, what he had meant when he confessed on those several occasions to fear. Why was such a man so often afraid? It must have begun to come to her now that there was one thing just such a man above all could be afraid of. He could be afraid of himself. His fear at all events was there; his fear was sweet to her, beautiful and tender

to her, was having coffee and buttered rolls and talk and laughter
that were no talk and laughter at all with her; his fear was in his
jesting postponing perverting voice. (ch. 30)

He is postponing telling her that he has a proposal to put to her,
a proposal that he can hardly articulate for shame.

'I'm talking to you in the most extraordinary way – I'm always
talking to you in the most extraordinary way, ain't I? One would
think you were about sixty and that I – I don't know what any one
would think *I* am. Unless a beastly cad!' he suggested. (ch. 30)

His proposal is that Maisie should agree to desert Mrs Wix –
betray her is Sir Claude's word for it – and live instead with the
illicit lovers to provide them with a cloak of respectability.

'My idea would be a nice little place – somewhere in the South –
where she and you would be together and as good as any one else.
And I should be as good too, don't you see? for I shouldn't live with
you, but I should be close to you – just round the corner, and it would
be just the same. My idea would be that it should all be perfectly open
and frank. *Honi soit qui mal y pense*, don't you know?' (ch. 30)

The burden of deciding all their futures is thus put on
Maisie's childish shoulders. The problem seems to her 'like an
impossible sum on a slate' and as she tries to put off the
moment when she must face the struggle to solve it she loses the
power to see:

She saw nothing that she had seen hitherto – no touch in the foreign
picture that had at first been always before her. The only touch was
that of Sir Claude's hand, and to feel her own in it was her mute
resistance to time. She went about as sightlessly as if he had been
leading her blindfold. (ch. 31)

Now she can only feel, and it is through feeling, working
blindfold at the problem that with her conscious mind she
believes she has postponed, that she finds an answer to the sum.
If Sir Claude will prove the singleness of his love for her by
giving up Mrs Beale she will match his sacrifice with the
answering sacrifice of Mrs Wix. The scene at the station, where
it seems, for a moment, that she has persuaded him to catch the
Paris train with her, though it shows her that after all she has

an answer to give him, also raises a further question about her much-loved companion. Why is he so afraid of himself when his temptations are so slight? Mrs Wix has already provided the answer, and now Maisie takes it in: 'he was afraid of his weakness – of his weakness'.

The extraordinary thing is that, perceiving this, she does not cease to love him, and nor do we want her to. Unlike Catherine Sloper or Isabel Archer, she does not feel deceived in her love. The Sir Claude she now sees so clearly is the Sir Claude she has always known, not the face of an unmasked stranger. But also, of course, she is protected by the magic armour of her youth. If she had been five years older she might have been able to get him on that train, but only at the cost of becoming like Mrs Beale, besides all the harm that so undependable a lover could do to a Maisie no longer under the protection of the gold Virgin. As for Sir Claude himself, he will show in the final scene how truly he understands the value of this small girl to whom he cannot lie without blushing, and in asserting the fineness of Maisie's moral sense will find the courage of his weakness and thus make moral sense of his own life.

At this point the principle of symmetry which has governed the novel leads to a remarkable *tour de force* that only James could have made to seem naturalistic. In Maisie's life, games have always been for adults; now the novel comes to an end with a scene that is patterned and stylized into a game. Earlier, when working out which 'side' each of the grown-ups was on, Maisie had reflected that it all seemed 'very much like puss-in-the-corner' and wondered 'if the distribution of parties would lead to a rushing to and fro and a changing of places'. In that taking of sides, 'Maisie of course, in such a delicate position, was on nobody's'; now she finds herself standing in the centre of the room while the three remaining adult players catch her in turn, until finally Sir Claude resolves the game by arranging the players in pairs, Maisie with Mrs Wix – 'Oh you're nobody' – and himself with Mrs Beale, to whom, with Maisie and Mrs Wix as 'solemn witnesses', he pledges his lifelong troth, with his weakness as the guarantee of his faithfulness. He will never give her up – because he can't. The algebraic problem has been resolved and they are all in the right relationships at last, mother and child, lover and lover: $(a+b)(x+y)$.

Only one touch is still needed to complete the novel. 'At last, in mid-channel, surrounded by the quiet sea', Maisie, now symbolically crossing from childhood to adolescence, tells Mrs Wix that Sir Claude had not been on the balcony to wave them goodbye. Mrs Wix's 'He went to *her*' receives the mysterious little reply, 'Oh I know!' Has Maisie at last discovered the great adult secret of sex? Like Mrs Wix, we can only wonder.

CHAPTER 6

The Awkward Age, The Ambassadors

In the first of his three great last novels, *The Ambassadors*, James returned to material that he had first used in a curious experimental novel written as a companion-piece to *What Maisie Knew*. The plot of *The Awkward Age* hinges on the return to the metropolis of an elderly man after thirty years of nursing a broken heart in the country and his being caught up, through the power of old associations, into a society of corrupt beautiful people. At the centre of that society is Mrs Brookenham, a devious enchantress, still, 'in her forty-first year', deceptively pretty:

She had about her the pure light of youth – would always have it; her head, her figure, her flexibility, her flickering colour, her lovely silly eyes, her natural quavering tone, all played together toward this effect by some trick that had never yet been exposed. (Bk ii ch. 1)

It is Mrs Brookenham's daughter Nanda, at eighteen the image of her dead grandmother, the beautiful Lady Julia he had long ago loved and lost, who attracts Mr Longdon's interest. Poor Nanda, guileless and innocent and far too young for her age, has all the same been tainted by the scandalous adult conversation which, banished far past the proper age to the schoolroom, she has in theory been protected from hearing. The devastating effect of this contamination on the poor girl's marriage prospects is compounded by her choosing to fall hopelessly in love with the man that her quietly rapacious mother also wants for herself.

Vanderbank, attractive, cold-hearted, discreetly on the make and as much too old for Nanda as he is too young for her mother, is contrasted with the warm-hearted but unfortunate Mitchy, fabulously wealthy shoemaker's son and frog prince, just as Nanda herself is contrasted with the absurdly cosseted little Aggie (her name, Agnesina, means little lamb) who has been kept artificially spotless by her thoroughly corrupt aunt, the better to marry her off to a large bag of money. Mitchy loves Nanda but marries Aggie who, once the constraints of her upbringing are removed, goes to the bad with startling rapidity in a desperate attempt to discover the identity of which that upbringing has deprived her. Nanda, vainly attempting to woo Vanderbank for herself, ends up, like Maisie with the Captain, trying to win him instead for her mother. Her 'Don't you still *like* mamma?' has only too much of Maisie's childish ring. The novel ends with Nanda choosing to leave the vicious labyrinth of London society for the peace of the country. Her tears at the loss of Vanderbank, 'a passion as sharp and brief as the flurry of a wild thing for an instant uncaged', seal her relationship with Mr Longdon, whose solemn kiss on her forehead claims her as adopted grand-daughter and chaste life-long companion.

Written almost entirely in dialogue and with a mannered wit at times reminiscent of a Restoration comedy, *The Awkward Age* is a remarkable technical achievement, but it has not worn well. It is not just that Nanda, pushing nineteen, has less intelligence and vitality than Maisie at half her age, nor even that Mr Longdon's old-maidish insistence that a thoroughly nice girl ought to think and speak, as well as look, like her own grandmother jars on the modern reader. Unfortunately for James, in *The Awkward Age* he was, without knowing it, documenting the beginning of a change in social mores which was to make his novel dated in little more than a decade. Though Mrs Brookenham's circle is a nasty-enough collection of spongers and fortune-hunters, the characters really demonstrate their immorality by such depravities as calling each other by nicknames – Vanderbank even, shockingly, once refers to Mrs Brookenham, whom he has known for ten years, by her christian name – using slang and reading 'bad books' in French. When in Virginia Woolf's first novel, *The Voyage Out*, completed in 1913, the heroine Rachel Vinrace, a thoroughly nice girl who has no difficulty whatever in getting engaged, asks her aunt, 'What are those women in Picadilly?' and gets the no-nonsense reply, 'They are prostitutes', the society of *The Awkward Age* is already on the way to becoming a fossil.

However, the interesting flawed experiment of a great writer is often merely a stage in a subterranean creative process. Like Richardson re-combining the elements of *Pamela* to produce the tragic grandeur of *Clarissa*, James was to perform the imaginative trick of transmuting *The Awkward Age* into *The Ambassadors*. All the pieces are there, the man of 55, the great city unvisited for thirty years, the powerful tug of old associations, the attractive young man halfway in age between a mother and a daughter and perceived as a quasi-stepson by the elderly visitor himself, the deceptively youthful enchantress, the docile, overprotected young girl – not even Nanda's tears or the yellow-covered French novels are missing, but all magically reordered into an authentic masterpiece. As with the coloured fragments ordered into a pattern by a kaleidoscope, the magic is done with mirrors. Memory, with its illusory doubling of experience, is the key to *The Ambassadors*.

This was the book which ushered in the greatest period of James's genius, a haunting comedy to be followed by a haunting tragedy and a final novel which takes us uncategoriz-ably beyond good and evil. It was James's own favourite among his novels, and it is possible that the emotional secret of the transformation of his material that enabled James to write it lies in the fact that he made his 55-year-old protagonist, like himself, an American and changed the setting to Paris, that city of his own youth. James, that most affectionate and generous of friends, was both a shy and an intensely private man. Tirelessly chronicling everything else that happened to him – a lunch of boiled eggs and bread-and-butter in a French inn, the death of a mulberry tree, the purchase of a Dachshund pup 'with a pedigree as long as a Remington ribbon' – he left his emotional life completely unrecorded. Despite the surmises, often lurid and intrusive, of biographers and critics, only one glimpse of it remains, a story – a fragment of a story – told by James to Edmund Gosse. 'He spoke of standing on the pavement of a city, in the dusk, and of gazing upwards across the misty street, watching, watching, for the lighting of a lamp in a window on the third storey.' We know neither the name of the city nor the name or sex of the 'unapproachable face', only that James stood for hours looking up at the lighted window that concealed it from him, wet with rain and weeping.

It is impossible to read that story without thinking of *The Ambassadors*, but it would be a mistake to suggest that the novel is in any obvious sense an autobiographical one. Whatever the private matters that we will never know about James, we know he was not Lambert Strether; and yet the book, for all its golden glow, breathes the chill spirit of a personal experience, and not for James alone. Stevie Smith, in her *Novel on Yellow Paper*, talks of Carroll's Alice who 'for one dreadful moment' is afraid she has turned into Mabel, and offers us an ironic reassurance. 'There are hazards enough in life and death, but Alice can never be Mabel.' Maybe not, and yet, novelist and readers alike, as we reach the age of fifty-five, may we live so long, and wake in the middle of the night to hear a small cold voice asking that terrible question, 'What have you done with your life?' we can none of us feel wholly certain of not being Lambert Strether.

As so often with James, the novel begins as a deceptively understated comedy. We feel a mild but sympathetic curiosity about this modestly attractive American tourist as he eases himself into the experience of Europe, a curiosity that quickens as he outlines to intelligent Maria Gostrey, in the appropriate setting of an evening at the theatre, the odd mission he has come on. It is a classically simple tale at this stage, with only three main characters, the admirable widowed mother, the ungrateful ne'er-do-well son and the anonymous, but all too imaginable, 'wicked woman' in Paris, and only one real motive, money – 'money, to very large amounts'. However, even before this tale is unfolded, as Strether enjoys his mildly romantic pre-theatre dinner with Maria Gostrey, a dinner 'face to face over a small table on which the lighted candles had rose-coloured shades', James already sounds an ominous note. Strether reflects on the odd fact that this is the first time he has ever dined alone with a lady 'at a public place before going to the play' and, apparently idly, asks himself why. It is only the particular way of putting the question that is novel; the answer comes with the weary readiness of things long taken for granted:

> He had married, in the far-away years, so young as to have missed the time natural in Boston for taking girls to the Museum; and it was absolutely true of him that – even after the close of the period of conscious detachment occupying the centre of his life, the grey middle desert of the two deaths, that of his wife and that, ten years later, of his boy – he had never taken anyone anywhere. (Bk II ch. 1)

The most important thing that Strether knows about himself is that 'the grey middle desert of the two deaths' has been the salient feature of the emotional geography of his life.

It was apropos of *The Ambassadors* that E. M. Forster wrote his famous and devastating description of James's characters:

> They are incapable of fun, of rapid motion, of carnality, and of nine-tenths of heroism. Their clothes will not take off, the diseases that ravage them are anonymous, like the sources of their income, their servants are noiseless or resemble themselves, no social explanation of the world we know is possible for them, for there are no stupid people in their world, no barriers of language, and no poor. Even their sensations are limited. They can land in Europe and look at works of art and at each other, but that is all. Maimed creatures can alone breathe in Henry James's pages – maimed yet specialized. They remind one of the exquisite deformities who haunted Egyptian art in the reign of Akhnaton – huge heads and tiny legs, but nevertheless charming. In the following reign they disappear.

As a piece of criticism this is both brilliant and appealing; though it loses some of its gloss if we apply it, say, to poor flaccid Mrs Tarrant, 'sustaining nature with a hard-boiled egg and a doughnut' as she waits for her appalling husband to come home, or poor grey greasy Mrs Wix in the 'glasses which, in humble reference to a divergent obliquity of vision, she called her straighteners, and a little ugly snuff-coloured dress trimmed with satin bands in the form of scallops and glazed with antiquity'. It is not only high art that is 'glazed with antiquity' for James; these particular poor and stupid people are characters that he knows from the inside; while as for the 'barriers of language', we have only to think of the moment when Maisie triumphantly overleaps them in the station at Boulogne:

It was the most extraordinary thing in the world: in the intensity of her excitement she not only by illumination understood all their French, but fell into it with an active perfection. She addressed herself straight to the porter.

'Prenny, prenny. Oh prenny!'   (ch. ·31)

   However, the really illuminating part of Forster's criticism is the idea that 'maimed creatures can alone breathe in Henry James's pages'. It is certainly true that of all James's characters only Felix and Gertrude could possibly be thought of as enjoying that mutually delighted and delighting physicality that lies behind Jane Austen's discreet phrase, 'perfect felicity'. For her, of course, perfect felicity was a door marked private, but it was not contemporary standards of taste alone that prevented James from taking his readers behind that door. Even late-nineteenth-century novelists were certainly denied the cheerful frankness which enables Richardson, for example, in *Sir Charles Grandison*, to show the ecstatic response of Charlotte's husband the first time he sees her breast-feeding their baby.

The wretch (trembling, however) pulled aside my handkerchief. I tried to scold; but was forced to press the little thing to me, to supply the place of the handkerchief – do you think I could not have killed him? – To be sure I was not half angry enough. I knew not what I did, you may well think – for I bowed my face on the smiling infant, who crowed to the pressure of my lip.
    Begone, Lord G–! said I – See! see! How shall I hold the little marmouset, if you devour first one of my hands, then the other.

(vol. vii letter 46)

But while it is impossible to imagine Celia in *Middlemarch*, say, writing such a letter to her best friend, it is equally hard to believe that contemporary readers had any difficulty in decoding the symbolism of the dramatic thunderstorm that accompanies the release of tension as Dorothea and Will fall into each other's arms. In James's novels it is different. Sexuality here is Isabel Archer running in terror from Caspar Goodwood's embrace, Olive Chancellor imagining Verena's faceless corpse, Sir Claude lying to Maisie about the stick he has left inside Mrs Beale's hotel bedroom. While we may not see these deformities as 'exquisite', Forster's comment does raise the crucial question, why are James's novels so full of the sexually stunted, the sexually warped, the sexually amputated? The answer, of course, lies in the very theme we have been exploring all along. Those intimately betrayed by the people they love best do indeed find themselves incapable of carnality and fun, and even, like Catherine Sloper, seating herself 'for life, as it were' with 'her morsel of fancy-work', of rapid motion. In his two final novels James goes on to show how this emotional disabling extends to the betrayers as well.

For Strether the case is rather different. By the end of the novel he will feel cheated enough, but the things that turned him into an emotional cripple happened a generation ago and the only betrayer was mortality itself. Always, 'beyond, behind' the 'dreadful cheerful sociable solitude' of his life is the haunting image of a family group, his wife, his son, himself, all of them ghosts:

the pale figure of his real youth, which held against its breast the two presences paler than itself... (Bk II ch. 2)

The death of his wife had exacted a terrible penalty for daring to love someone, and the subsequent death of his son, with its disabling legacy of guilt inextricably mixed with regret, exacted a still more terrible penalty for daring to grieve for that loss:

He had again and again made out for himself that he might have kept his little boy, his little dull boy who had died at school of rapid diphtheria, if he had not in those years so insanely given himself to merely missing the mother. It was the soreness of his remorse that the child had in all likelihood not really been dull – had been dull, as he had been banished and neglected, mainly because the father had been unwittingly selfish. This was doubtless but the secret habit of sorrow, which had slowly given way to time; yet there remained an ache sharp enough to make the spirit, at the sight now and again of some fair young man just growing up, wince with the thought of an opportunity lost. Had ever a man, he had finally fallen into the way of asking himself, lost so much and even done so much for so little? (Bk II ch. 2)

After that, he had decided not to feel, a decision which entailed embracing failure 'in everything' as a way of life. Like the inhabitants of Eliot's *Waste Land*, 'feeding a little life with dried tubers', he retreated into the only comfort offered by the grey desert, the comfort of emotional sterility. It is the long habit of this frame of mind which has led him to accept Mrs Newsome's proposal that he should win her hand in marriage (and the considerable cash benefits that go with it) by performing the demeaning task of persuading his future stepson, with the double bribe of a considerable income and a virgin bride, to desert his mercenary French mistress. Now he is in Paris in the spring, which, like April in *The Waste Land*, 'stirring dull roots with spring rain', has made something begin to come painfully alive in him:

Buried for long years in dark corners... these few germs had sprouted again under forty-eight hours of Paris.   (Bk II ch. 2)

It is typical of poor Strether that the first form this resurrection takes is an intellectual one and that what makes it painful when it ought to be delightful is irrational puritan guilt. Starved for half a lifetime of the excitements of imaginative literature – in Woollett the life of the mind, as represented by Mrs Newsome and the review he edits on her behalf, is restricted to economics, politics and ethics – he is irresistibly drawn to the bookshop windows, but, in an absurd sublimation of the protestant work ethic, despite his 'hungry gazes through clear plates behind which lemon-coloured volumes were as fresh as fruit on the tree' his conscience forbids him the purchase of one of these enticing books until he has made contact with Chad. He already suspects that his own reborn capacity for enjoyment is an eating of forbidden fruit which will tempt him away from the moral austerity necessary to carry out his mission. It is not merely the lemon-coloured volumes but Paris itself which is conspiring to seduce him:

It hung before him this morning, the vast bright Babylon, like some huge iridescent object, a jewel brilliant and hard, in which parts were not to be discriminated nor differences comfortably marked. It twinkled and trembled and melted together, and what seemed all surface one moment seemed all depth the next.   (Bk II ch. 2)

He has entered a world of appearances, bewildering, sensuous and infinitely appealing after the hard, plain moral certainties of Woollett.

To the reader, of course, these certainties appear even plainer and considerably less moral than they do to poor Strether. Woollett is a cultural matriarchy – high-minded, narrow and smug – financed by the proceeds of dubious business practices and ruthless industrial piracy. It is quite in line with the values of such a society that a young man like Chad should sow his sexual wild oats in Europe before coming home to a respectable marriage with a suitably blameless girl, but quite out of line that such sexual on-goings should take precedence over sound commercial interests. To the prurient puritan imagination of Woollett, though of course it would never utter such a word, any woman who comes between a young man and the family business can be little better than a whore. This underlying idea, with its unexamined confusion between moral concerns and money concerns, will play its part in leading Strether astray, a process that begins before he even sets eyes on Chad.

In effect, a trap is set, 'the most baited, the most gilded of traps', and Strether, though perceptive enough to suspect its existence, falls into it all the same. Though the inflexibly truthful Mrs Newsome has promised not to inform her son of Strether's imminent arrival, perhaps her less scrupulous daughter Sarah – a moral thug to Mrs Newsome's 'moral swell' – has taken it upon herself to do so. At all events, Chad is diplomatically out of town, having lent his charmingly luxurious apartment to exactly the kind of friend best calculated to mollify his mother's emissary. Bilham, the 'little artist man' who has given up painting – exposed to the fatal charms of Paris, his 'productive powers' have 'faltered in proportion as his knowledge grew' – is in some ways a younger version of Strether himself, but for his serene exemption from puritan guilt (as Strether tells Waymarsh, *he* doesn't come from Boston). He is an artist now only in the sense of being an observer, and his disingenuous friendship fosters in Strether the wistful idea that he too, so late in life, could turn responsiveness to experience into an art form.

Both Bilham and Chad, in their different ways, are expatriate American specimens of that very Parisian phenomenon, the *flâneur*. Idler, stroller, observer of life, ideally rich enough to be a dandy and, if not an artist himself, at least the friend and associate of artists, the *flâneur* made doing nothing into a distinguished life style. It is a life style inconceivable in Woollett, yet early in his Parisian adventure Strether is already discovering a potential for it in himself:

I stayed, I dawdled, I trifled; above all I looked round. I saw, in fine; and – I don't know what to call it – I sniffed.   (Bk iii ch. 1)

James, in his late novels, has been accused of analysing over-subtly the minutiae of experience, but in *The Ambassadors* it is, of course, not James but poor Strether who does that, blinding himself in the process to facts that in the end will be all too brutally plain to him. Even his own cultural background conspires to betray him – it is hard for a man reared on the values of Boston to believe that the beautiful and the good are not synonymous. At any rate, when Chad at last makes his calculatedly theatrical entrance, Strether is so bowled over by his superficial charm and polish that he fails to reflect that knowing how to enter a box is, after all, a trivial accomplishment which sheds no light at all on the real worth of its possessor. The painful longings stirred into life by Strether's return to Paris play their part here too. The oafish Chad, thus miraculously transformed, becomes a symbolic replacement for the 'little dull boy' whose loss makes his father wince at the sight of a 'fair young man just growing up'. Later, Strether's identification with him will become closer still. He would like to *be* Chad, with the inevitable consequence that he comes to see Chad only in terms of what he himself would like to be.

Just as Chad delays his entrance into the novel, so too does Madame de Vionnet, and while she does so little Bilham provides Strether with a crucial piece of misinformation: the relationship which is holding Chad in Paris is 'a virtuous attachment'. To understand the full impact of this we have to return to Forster's assessment of James's characters: 'there are no stupid people in their world, no barriers of language, and no poor.' By the end of the novel Strether will have discovered his own stupidity and condemned himself to poverty, and he will also have become what makes all of us poor and stupid in the end – he will have become old; and these things will have happened to him because he has entered a foreign world, not in any sense 'his' despite the potent memories it awakes in him, a world whose language he fails to understand. Terms that seem to him like the common currency of Boston – virtuous, beautiful, good – mean something treacherously different here, though the associated word 'wonderful', with its faint if appealing suggestions of the alarming and the illicit, goes some way towards bridging the culture gap.

Madame de Vionnet, to whom that adjective supremely belongs, confuses him still further when she does finally appear. Misled by the Woollett idea of her as 'base, venal – out of the streets', he is unable to believe that a 'wicked woman' could be so much like the respectable women back home. Madame de Vionnet, with far more to lose than Chad, who merely wants to please himself rather than his family, is putting on a show for Strether, but here again his ignorance of a cultural language plays a crucial part in the deception. Unfamiliar with a society in which the *monde* and the *demi-monde* can mingle, he is unable to imagine that an adulteress could be addressed by a duchess as 'Ma toute-belle'. His acquaintance with the lemon-coloured volumes has not extended to Colette, whose first novel, *Claudine à l'école*, disguised under the name of her husband, the deplorable Willy, must have been in those enticing bookshop windows; and even if it had, Colette herself was still preoccupied with schoolgirl sexuality and memories of her rural childhood, though doubtless Strether would have found the innocent frankness of her novel shocking enough.

Strether, in his rôle of innocent abroad, is more like presexual Maisie than knowing, adolescent Claudine. Like Maisie, too, he revels in the experience of France, but where she proudly deployed her handful of French words – a tiny vocabulary, consisting 'mainly of the names of dishes', whose use made her feel confident and in possession of this new, foreign world   Strether, despite his good reading-knowledge of French, feels too self-conscious to speak it:

He had been afraid of Chad and of Maria and of Madame de Vionnet; he had been most of all afraid of Waymarsh, in whose presence, so far as they had mixed together in the light of the town,

he had never without somehow paying for it aired either his
vocabulary or his accent.   (Bk xi ch. 3)

This disabling fear of really taking the language into his mouth
and possessing it symbolizes his wider dilemma. It is not just
because his surmises are naïvely romantic that he gets things so
horribly wrong, but also because they are timid. Strether the
observer, as he ponders the nature of Chad's virtuous
attachment, is dangerously close to being a voyeur. He tries to
avert that danger by blotting sex out of the story he tells himself
about Chad and Madame de Vionnet. Really he doesn't want
to understand their language and when, in the end, he is forced
to, the unwelcome knowledge makes him feel, with shame, that
'he had dressed the possibility in vagueness, as a little girl might
have dressed her doll'. The innocence which clad Maisie in
magic armour has betrayed Strether, and this is not to be
wondered at. The real source of Maisie's inviolability is
touched on in passing in the scene where Mrs Beale arrives in
Boulogne – without, among her luggage, any 'appurtenance of
Sir Claude's':

She knew his dressing-bag now – oh with the fondest knowledge! –
and there was an instant during which its not being there was a stroke
of the worst news. She was yet to learn what it could be to recognize
in some lapse of a sequence the proof of an extinction, and therefore
remained unaware that this momentary pang was a foretaste of the
experience of death.   (ch. 27)

Strether has lost that particular virginity long ago, and
innocence for him now is a frightened bandaging of the eyes
against reality. Chad and Madame de Vionnet create for him
the illusion that he is the spectator of his own lost youth, played
out for him as if on a stage by a pair of consummate actors.
Willingly he suspends his disbelief.

There is even a moment when he confronts the fact that this
is what he is doing. The real victim of the novel is Jeanne de
Vionnet, docile and dominated as Pansy Osmond before her
but with the added pathos that she has been taught to declare
that she is free:

'Oh but I'm almost American too. That's what mamma has wanted me to be – I mean *like* that; for she has wanted me to have lots of freedom. She has known such good results from it.'   (Bk VI ch. 2)

Strether sees her vulnerability but distances himself from it by treating her as an art object:

She was fairly beautiful to him – a faint pastel in an oval frame: he thought of her already as of some lurking image in a long gallery, the portrait of a small old-time princess of whom nothing was known but that she had died young.   (Bk VI ch. 2)

Seeing the world of the novel entirely through Strether's eyes, the reader can indeed get no closer to Jeanne than the bare facts of her pathetic fate – not to die young, but to be married off, with the active connivance of her mother's lover, with whom, in all probability, she is quietly and hopelessly in love, to appease her mother's jealousy. Strether himself bears some of the blame for this – Madame de Vionnet, early in their acquaintance, has employed him to find out whether Jeanne is in love with Chad, and, in attempting to persuade her to let the question rest, he has inadvertently answered it. He is shocked by Madame de Vionnet's bald statement, 'We're marrying Jeanne' – 'that wasn't the way Jeanne should be married' – but really to feel how coldly she is being sacrificed would be to destroy the dream of the past for which – as the avenging arrival of Sarah Pocock has made abundantly clear – he is almost certainly going to have to pay with the whole of his future:

He had allowed for depths, but these were greater: and it was as if, oppressively – indeed absurdly – he was responsible for what they had now thrown up to the surface. It was – through something ancient and cold in it – what he would have called the real thing. In short his hostess's news, though he couldn't have explained why, was a sensible shock, and his oppression a weight he felt he must somehow or other immediately get rid of. There were too many connections missing to make it tolerable that he should do anything else. He was prepared to suffer – before his own inner tribunal – for Chad; he was prepared to suffer even for Madame de Vionnet. But he wasn't prepared to suffer for the little girl. So now having said the proper thing, he wanted to get away.

Strether's suffering, when the time comes, for Chad and Madame de Vionnet will have in it an element of retribution for this particular refusal to care and to feel.

By now the fresh springtime of the start of the novel has turned to 'hot and dusty' summer and Strether is desperately playing for time; staving off the aggressive onslaughts of Sarah Pocock, who refuses to believe in Chad's wonderful trans-formation; assuaging his residual uneasiness about Jeanne by encouraging little Bilham to propose to Maimie; putting off the moment when he will have to make up his mind whose side he is on; putting off the day when – bleak prospect – he will have to go home. Winter is coming and Strether, the improvident grasshopper, will have to return to the ant society of Woollett with nothing to live on but his memories. Nervously he tries to garner a few more for the coming time of want. Meanwhile, the strain of acting out Strether's platonic idea of a virtuous attachment is beginning to tell on Chad and Madame de Vionnet, whose relationship, already under threat before Strether's arrival, is crumbling further as Chad muses on the business opportunities he is ostensibly so ready to relinquish. Maria Gostrey tries to warn Strether that the lovers have simply had enough of him:

'Mr Newsome and Madame de Vionnet may, as we were saying, leave town. How long do you think you can bear it without them?'

Strether's reply to this was at first another question. 'Do you mean in order to get away from me?'

Her answer had an abruptness. 'Don't find me rude if I say I should think they'd want to.'   (Bk xi ch. 2)

Once again he refuses to understand. 'You mean after what they've done to me?' Soon, though, he is going to have to understand. Under the pressure of their separate needs both Strether and the lovers arrange a modest excursion into the past, and it is this attempt to escape for a little from their various predicaments that leads to a convergence which, literally, puts Strether into the picture at last.

Strether's past, as we have already seen, is treacherous territory, but this particular small expanse of it seems harmless enough. His first idyll on returning to Paris had been with the lemon-coloured volumes he had failed to read as a young man; this final one is with the painting he had failed to buy, 'a certain small Lambinet that had charmed him, long years before, at a Boston dealers''. The story of his encounter with this painting is the story of his life in miniature:

> It had been offered, he remembered, at a price he had been instructed to believe the lowest ever named for a Lambinet, a price he had never felt so poor as on having to recognize, all the same, as beyond a dream of possibility. He had dreamed – had turned and twisted possibilities for an hour: it had been the only adventure of his life in connexion with the purchase of a work of art. (Bk xi ch. 3)

The painting, 'absurdly never forgotten', has long since gone out of fashion; now Strether wants to make it new again by taking his memory of it back into the French countryside which it depicted:

> to assist at the restoration to nature of the whole far-away hour: the dusty day in Boston, the background of the Fitchburg Depot, of the maroon-coloured sanctum, the special-green vision, the ridiculous price, the poplars, the willows, the rushes, the river, the sunny silvery sky, the shady woody horizon. (Bk xi ch. 3)

Lambinet, who has never come back into fashion, was a member of the Barbizon school, along with Corot and Millet and with the American painter William Morris Hunt who taught both the young Henry James and his brother William before the Civil War, the time when the future, for Americans, seemed so full of promise and when Strether too was young. Strether's fate has always been to see the most modest ambitions and opportunities slip away from him, but this one comes to meet him with an almost ominous alacrity:

> the train pulled up just at the right spot and he found himself getting out as securely as if to keep an appointment. (Bk xi ch. 3)

He has stepped through the picture-frame into the dangerous world of art, which initially appears to him to be a world of appearances mixed with memory:

> The oblong gilt frame disposed its enclosing lines; the poplars and willows, the reeds and river – a river of which he didn't know, and didn't want to know, the name – fell into a composition, full of

felicity, within them; the sky was silver and turquoise and varnish; the village on the left was white and the church on the right was grey; it was all there, in short – it was what he wanted: it was Tremont Street, it was France, it was Lambinet.   (Bk xi ch. 3)

This is an idyll indeed, but again the ominous note sounds, and a little louder this time, as Strether walks deeper into the picture:

making for the shady woody horizon and boring so deep into his impression and his idleness that he might fairly have got through them again and reached the maroon-coloured wall.   (Bk xi ch. 3)

Before the day is over he will have learnt that art, like life, offers us nostalgic fictions only to ambush us with the shocking immediacy of truth.

Henry James first encountered the Impressionist painters in 1876 and, though perceptive about their aims, was initially rather shocked by their work:

The beautiful, to them, is what the supernatural is to the Positivists – a metaphysical notion, which can only get one into a muddle and is to be severely let alone. Let it alone, they say, and it will come at its own pleasure; the painter's proper field is simply the actual, and to give a vivid impression of how a thing happens to look, at a particular moment, is the essence of his mission.   (*The Painter's Eye*, p. 114)

This substitution of 'unadorned reality' for the 'arrangement, embellishment, selection' which seemed to him the true business of an artist struck him as a kind of cynicism. Later he came not only to admire these painters but to copy their effects. In *What Maisie Knew* he created the brilliant impression of 'how things happen to look' through the fresh eyes of a completely unsated observer. Now, in *The Ambassadors*, he does something bolder and more shocking, adding a single detail to Strether's painting and so giving it an immediacy that could indeed be the work of a cynic. The detail, the little dab of colour which suddenly makes the painting both new and complete, is a pink parasol, and the artist is that uncaring fate who sits at the crossroads where human paths intersect.

Coincidences in novels often feel a bit contrived; this one has all the slow-motion inevitability of appalling chance encounters in real life. One moment Strether is looking at a painting, the next he is watching Chad and Madame de Vionnet, who have sneaked away from Paris for a mercifully Stretherless illicit weekend in the country, come floating towards him down that river whose name he didn't want to know and debating, as they do so, whether they can get away with rowing right on downstream as if their dear old friend were not there. It is a moment of pure nightmare, and it is also – poor Strether – a moment of high comedy. There follow fake surprise, false protestations of delight, a shared meal, a shared journey back to Paris, embarrassment and lies. Strether feels most of the embarrassment and Madame de Vionnet tells most of the lies, while Chad leans back and lets her get on with it:

> He habitually left things to others, as Strether was so well aware …
> (Bk xi ch. 4)

Madame de Vionnet – an actress since her schooldays – has played a series of rôles for Strether, from the deliberately low-key and respectable young beauty at Gloriani's party through thoughtful friend and anxious mother to inheritrix of Napoleonic glories and secular saint, and each time she has dressed for the part. Now, with her pink parasol and not even a shawl to cover her shoulders, she chatters feverishly in French, attempting, quite as if it were possible, to hide the shivering and naked truth which she knows that Strether can see perfectly well:

> Her shawl and Chad's overcoat and her other garments, and his, those they had each worn the day before, were at the place, best known to themselves – a quiet retreat enough, no doubt – at which they had been spending the twenty-four hours, to which they had fully meant to return that evening, from which they had so remarkably swum into Strether's ken, and the tacit repudiation of which had been thus the essence of her comedy.   (Bk xi ch. 4)

Strether has woken from his dream of a nobly sublimated sexuality to find himself peering through a bedroom keyhole. The furtively abandoned garments that he sees there fill him with as much shame as any vision of entwined and naked bodies could have done, and the most shameful thing of all is the realization that his devastating discovery is only of what everyone else has known all along.

The dream is over, but the play is not. Madame de Vionnet has one rôle left, for which, as if to efface the memory of the pink parasol, she dresses in white with a black gauze scarf like Madame Roland on the scaffold; but this deliberate pathos breaks down into real gasping, sobbing grief when Strether – who has begun to learn the language at last – says to her, 'You're afraid for your life!' As she weeps, 'as vulgarly troubled, in very truth, as a maidservant crying for her young man', Strether is thinking not of her but of 'the passion, mature, abysmal, pitiful, she represented' and of the strangeness that she should feel all this for Chad:

She had but made Chad what he was – so why could she think she had made him infinite? She had made him better, she had made him best, she had made him anything one would; but it came to our friend with supreme queerness that he was none the less only Chad.

(Bk xii ch. 2)

A middle-aged woman desperately clutching at a cooling lover ten years younger and ambitious for new experiences, Madame de Vionnet has sacrificed her daughter and seduced and ruined poor credulous Strether, who has had only a tête-à-tête over an omelette and a bottle of Chablis to show for it, and all for nothing. Strether, if he had chosen, could have known the truth all along; little Bilham had explained Chad's feelings to him plainly enough. 'You see he's not happy ... He wants to be free. He isn't used, you see, to being so good.' This is the moment, as he watches her weeping, when Strether at last makes his choice. He has idealized and idolized this abject woman whom he now never wants to see again – and he still does. With shame and pity he promises to try to help her one last time.

Thus it is that Strether finds himself playing the most demeaning rôle of all, the aged pandar wearily climbing Chad's stairs at midnight to urge that spoilt, successful young man to stay with his outworn mistress. There has always been something about the ring of Chad's name which failed to fit with his wonderful transformation. Now, as he crudely declares, 'I give you my word of honour that I'm not a bit tired of her', we realize what it is. The high but superficial polish which Madame de Vionnet has given him has merely turned him from a lout into a cad. The rôle of *flâneur* which he had apparently learnt so flawlessly is in origin an aristocratic one, based on the French admiration for the sang-froid of the English gentleman. Now he is reverting to type – the type of his father and grandfather – but all the same he is an artist in a way and, as he recounts to Strether, he has just discovered his *métier*. We never discover the identity of the 'small, trivial, rather ridiculous object of the commonest domestic use' which the Newsome factory produces, but homely Jim Pocock has let out that the great business opportunity to which Chad is summoned is 'to go back and boss the advertising'. Now Chad has begun to make enquiries about advertising and come up with a very twentieth-century discovery. 'It's an art like another, and infinite like all the arts ... In the hands, naturally, of a master.'

We have forgotten about the small, trivial object in the course of the novel. Initially just a teasing riddle for the reader – toothbrush? shoe-horn? safety-pin? none of them seems quite to fit the description – it now comes back with a new and alarming significance. Advertising is the art of selling not the product itself but the ambience which, in the hands of a master, can be created around the product. It is the art, in other words, of appearances, the art that Madame de Vionnet has so successfully taught to Chad. It is for that vulgar little object of 'the commonest domestic use' that Strether has thrown away his future.

The little unnamed article comes explicitly back into the novel in the final scene, in which Maria Gostrey offers Strether a future after all. There is a curious serenity about Strether now as he reports to Maria Chad's unconvincing protestations and promises, the serenity with which the old survey a world for which they have ceased to take any responsibility. Chad, after all that Madame de Vionnet and Strether have done for him, is still 'the son of his father' and there is nothing more that Strether can do except return to Woollett and the nothing that awaits him there. It is at this point that Maria holds out to him, in her tacit offer 'of exquisite service, of lightened care, for the rest of his days', the possibility of a life as simple, full and perfect as the 'small ripe round melon' on the breakfast table, a life in which appearances could be trusted because it would rest 'all so firm, on selection. And what ruled selection was beauty and knowledge.' Instead of the dazzling, transient, deceptive immediacy of the Impressionist painting we have a Dutch interior, ordered and rational but suffused with a light in which intellect and feeling can become one and be at peace, the cool clear light of every day blessing the solid objects it touches. It is the New England aesthetic restored to its European origins, and it offers Strether a life he could no more accept than, seeing her clearly at last, he could go back and marry Mrs Newsome. He has had his own vision of beauty, shifting, seductive, treacherous, compelling and shallow, and now it is time to go home. For a moment he searches for a formula which will allow him to refuse, without slighting it, Maria's patient, intelligent love. She, at least, is someone with whom he has a language in common, the Boston language of high moral seriousness travestied by Sarah Pocock and Mrs Newsome. He is turning her down, he tells her at last, for the sake of altruism, 'Not, out of the whole affair, to have got anything for myself' – except, of course, as she hastens to remind him, for his 'wonderful impressions'.

CHAPTER 7

The Wings of the Dove

She waited, Kate Croy, for her father to come in ...

James concentrates our attention at the beginning of *The Wings of the Dove*, as he did at the beginning of *The Portrait of a Lady*, on the striking figure of a handsome girl dressed in black; appropriately so, since this is the novel in which he returns to the theme of that earlier girl rashly 'affronting her destiny' and gives it what he himself would call an extra turn of the screw. Like *Portrait*, this is to be a novel about betrayal, and it begins with the sick familiar taste of distrust and frustration and the recoil of physical disgust.

She waited, Kate Croy ...

The inversion in those opening words tells us that the action has already become wearisome to the actress long before the rise of the curtain reveals her to the audience. It speaks too of her determination not to be defeated. The place where she waits, the 'vulgar little room', in which her senses cringe away from contact with any of the surfaces – 'slippery', 'sticky', 'sallow', 'wanting in freshness' – which surround her, is the outward embodiment of the relationship which holds her there, her relationship with her father. Only one surface is a release from the oppressive grip of that relationship: the tarnished surface of the mirror. As she gazes into it, the reader, looking over her shoulder, sees her face. It is only in this way that we *can* see the full significance of that face. At this early stage, the centre of consciousness of the novel is located inside Kate, and Kate is not merely admiring her own beauty, she is summoning up her forces, surveying her chief weapon in a fight in which she alone has not fallen.

Apart from the striking central figure, the start of the novel could not be more unlike the start of *Portrait*. The great house, the mellow sunlight, the spread of velvet lawn, the group of assorted male figures all ready to turn and witness the entrance of the heroine into her novel, have all contracted to this sordid little room. There is another difference too, but one that the reader (the platonic reader, who comes to the novel untouched by blurbs or hearsay or the reading of critical books like this one) has no way of knowing yet. It is not, in fact, the heroine of the novel who is waiting for her father to come in. The reader, unsuspecting, responds to her with the sympathetic curiosity appropriate to a heroine.

As she waits, this beautiful girl dressed in mourning black, she is certainly behaving like a heroine. She is musing on the downfall of her house. The father who presently enters is a part of that downfall. Lionel Croy bears a close resemblance to 'the late Mr Archer', remembered with such pride by Isabel but noted among 'the large number of those to whom he owed money' for possessing 'a remarkably handsome head and a very taking manner (indeed, as one of them had said, he was always taking something)'; but while Mr Archer is sketched in with a few broad comic strokes, Lionel Croy is a finished portrait of hypocrisy who would not seem out of place in Dickens' *Bleak House*. Although he only enters the novel twice, he is an important character both strategically and symbolically. At this early stage he serves to draw closer together the net of circumstances in which Kate is trapped. His symbolic function becomes clear much later, when his unseen presence adds its force to one of the crucial scenes of the book.

Kate, unlike Isabel, has no illusions about her father, and yet, as we quickly discover, she has come to offer to live with him in the 'vulgar little room' which is all his protection would afford her, sharing with him a part of her small inheritance from her dead mother (the rest has gone to help support her widowed sister Marian and a brood of small nephews and nieces) and abandoning for his sake a rich and childless aunt who seems bent on adopting her. Mr Croy repudiates her offer with violence. Her aunt, Mrs Lowder, is her duty and her fortune, a fortune in which both her father and her sister feel themselves to have a personal interest. He has no doubt, either, about the motivation of her offer. Kate is in love, and with some penniless young man. 'Who *is* the beggarly sneak?' he asks her.

We meet Merton Densher, the penniless young man, at the start of the second book of the novel. Again we find ourselves happy to take a sympathetic interest in him, although in his case the warning signs are clearer. We first glimpse him as a 'longish, leanish, fairish young Englishman' wandering, apparently aimlessly, in Kensington Gardens on a winter afternoon; but it is not simply the deceptive appearance of daytime leisure (being a journalist, he works at night) which makes his profession so hard for an observer to pin down:

He was young for the House of Commons, he was loose for the Army. He was refined, as might have been said, for the City and, quite apart from the cut of his cloth, sceptical, it might have been felt, for the Church. On the other hand he was credulous for diplomacy, or perhaps even for science, while he was perhaps at the same time too much in his mere senses for poetry and yet too little in them for art. You would have got fairly near him by making out in his eyes the potential recognition of ideas; but you would have quite fallen away again on the question of the ideas themselves. The difficulty with Densher was that he looked vague without looking weak – idle without looking empty. (Bk II ch. 1)

In many ways this is an appealing description – Densher is attractive, as well as elusive, enough to cause passers-by to speculate about him, and the reader is intrigued and wants to discover what he is really like. Yet this description of a man who could almost be any number of things and in fact succeeds in being none of them conveys a damaging sense of an intellect failing to bring itself to bear on anything substantial. Densher 'looked vague without looking weak – idle without looking empty', and yet vagueness lies a little too close to weakness, as idleness does to emptiness, and to have to say of a man that he does not appear weak or empty is to suggest that there might be a danger that he could be taken to be both. But these are the doubts of hindsight, the discoveries of the second-time reader for whom the novel offers a fine web of implications and ironies. The first-time reader is disposed to take him on trust.

He is not, of course, really wandering aimlessly when we encounter him in Kensington Gardens, but awaiting a rendezvous with Kate. This is their regular meeting-place, chosen with a mixture of discretion and defiance, since Densher is not approved of by Kate's aunt Mrs Lowder, in whose house in Lancaster Gate, overlooking the park, Kate is now living. It is through Kate's confidences in him here that we learn the full extent of the family downfall by which she is trapped:

the dishonour her father had brought them, his folly and cruelty and wickedness; the wounded state of her mother, abandoned despoiled and helpless, yet, for the management of such a home as remained to them, dreadfully unreasonable too; the extinction of her two young brothers – one, at nineteen, the eldest of the house, by typhoid fever contracted at a poisonous little place, as they had afterwards found out, that they had taken for a summer; the other, the flower of the flock, a middy on the *Britannia*, dreadfully drowned, and not even by an accident at sea, but by cramp, unrescued, while bathing, too late in the autumn, in a wretched little river during a holiday visit to the home of a shipmate. Then Marian's unnatural marriage, in itself a kind of spiritless turning of the other cheek to fortune: her actual wretchedness and plaintiveness, her greasy children, her impossible claims... (Bk II ch. 1)

'Not even by an accident at sea' – it is the meanness and smallness of the 'wretched little river' and the 'poisonous little place' which make those deaths terrible by making them comic, stripping them of the dignity of tragedy. Even the misery of the survivors is tainted by unreasonableness and a 'spiritless turning of the other cheek to fortune'. And behind it all lies a secret: the 'impossible thing', never spoken of, never revealed, that her father has done.

Kate herself is a survivor of a different kind, sharp, clever, beautiful and determined. All the same, the family failure has left its mark on her. For Kate, poverty has the taste of dishonour and defeat, and Merton Densher is poor; worse, it is

quite evident that he will never be anything else. Kate has tried
to throw herself off the cliff and failed. A life of poverty with her
father would soon have driven her into Densher's arms; a life
of luxury with Aunt Maud has a very different effect on her,
even though she perceives it to be also a life of captivity.

James shows us Maud Lowder's character, through
Densher's eyes, in terms of the contents of her house in
Lancaster Gate:

He had never dreamed of anything so fringed and scalloped, so
buttoned and corded, drawn everywhere so tight and curled
everywhere so thick. He had never dreamed of so much gilt and glass,
so much satin and plush, so much rosewood and marble and
malachite. But it was above all the solid forms, the wasted finish, the
misguided cost, the general attestation of morality and money, a good
conscience and a big balance. These things finally represented for him
a portentous negation of his own world of thought... (Bk ii ch. 2)

Mrs Lowder, vulgar, florid, powerful and extremely wealthy,
plans to unite her dead husband's money (acquired in trade)
with a title by marrying Kate to an impoverished aristocrat,
Lord Mark. In this plan she acknowledges her sense of Kate's
quality. Kate is her 'investment', and as she tells Densher,

'I want to see her high, high up – high up and in the light.'

This is no contest between an equally determined man and
woman for ownership of a passive girl, as in *The Bostonians*. If
anything, the contest is between Kate herself and Mrs Lowder.
They are well-matched opponents. Kate is neither florid nor
vulgar, but all the same there is a strong family likeness
between aunt and niece. However, there is another kind of
conflict going on inside Kate herself; she is strongly drawn to
Mrs Lowder's world of money (as well as being shoved towards
it by her father and sister) but just as strongly drawn to
Densher's 'world of thought'. She sees him, in a reversal of the
story of Adam and Eve of which the irony will only be apparent
later, as 'having tasted of the tree and being thereby prepared
to assist her to eat'. His cosmopolitan childhood, 'his Swiss
schools, his German university', his mother who had 'copied,
patient lady, famous pictures in great museums', all make him

seem to her the real intellectual thing, brilliant and 'com-
plicated'. But Kate wants to taste the fruit of Densher's tree
while still contriving to have Aunt Maud's cake. She persuades
Densher that they should conceal their engagement for a while
– Aunt Maud can perhaps be 'squared' – and Densher, though
unable to see how the 'squaring' can possibly take effect, gives
in the more willingly because his newspaper has just asked him
to spend the next few months in America.

I have spent so much time on these opening chapters because
it is the triangle of forces established here (a situation which
would have been material enough in itself for one of James's
earlier fictions) which determines the chain of reactions that
starts to take place when, at the beginning of Book Three, the
true heroine finally enters her novel. She enters it almost
incognito, as one of two ladies making their way, in the early
spring, from the Italian lakes to the Swiss Alps. We first saw
Kate Croy in close-up and through her own eyes. We first see
Milly Theale from a distance, and when we draw closer to her
it is through the eyes of her companion, Mrs Stringham, that
we focus on her. This is no accident; all through the book Milly
is to be an image, even a fantasy-figure, in the eyes and minds
of others. Mrs Stringham is a cultured New England lady living
in Boston, middle-class, middle-aged, widowed and childless, a
contributor of romantic short stories to 'the best magazines'.
She looks at Milly from the first with a fiction-writer's eye; to
her, Milly is 'the real thing, the romantic life itself':

the slim, constantly pale, delicately haggard, anomalously, agreeably
angular young person, of not more than two-and-twenty summers, in
spite of her marks, whose hair was somehow exceptionally red even
for the real thing, which it innocently confessed to being, and whose
clothes were remarkably black even for robes of mourning, which was
the meaning they expressed. It was New York mourning, it was New
York hair, it was a New York history, confused as yet, but
multitudinous, of the loss of parents, brothers, sisters, almost every
human appendage, all on a scale and with a sweep that had required
the greater stage; it was a New York legend of affecting, of romantic
isolation, and, beyond everything, it was by most accounts, in respect
to the mass of money so piled on the girl's back, a set of New York
possibilities. She was alone, she was stricken, she was rich, and in
particular was strange...   (Bk III ch. 1)

Already we begin to see the ironic paralleling of Kate and Milly which is to lead to the savage symmetries of the catastrophe. Milly, like Kate, is dressed in mourning. Kate has lost a mother, two brothers and a brother-in-law, but that does not make her a romantic heroine. It is the money which gives the deaths of Milly's relatives their legendary glow. The 'free-living ancestors, handsome dead cousins, lurid uncles, beautiful vanished aunts' have all left Milly money, so much money that it has become like the air she breathes, something she no longer even notices:

> She couldn't dress it away, nor walk it away, nor read it away, nor think it away; she could neither smile it away in any dreamy absence nor blow it away in any softened sigh. She couldn't have lost it if she had tried – that was what it was to be really rich.   (Bk III ch. 1)

To high-thinking, plain-living Mrs Stringham, the least mercenary of women, Milly's friendship is an explosion of colour into a grey life. Milly is her princess, and when the princess asks her to depart in haste for a lengthy tour of Europe she agrees without a second thought.

This initial presentation of Milly to the reader through Mrs Stringham's consciousness makes it impossible for us to judge whether Milly is really something rich and strange or simply an ordinary and rather neurotic young woman falsely gilded by the light her own wealth casts on her and by Mrs Stringham's need for a real-life heroine to embody and surpass the heroines of her fiction. If Milly, odd-looking angular Milly, is truly as beautiful as Mrs Stringham thinks her then she is a paragon indeed, yet those beauties may be no more than the subtleties of her observer's imagination:

> She had arts and idiosyncrasies of which no great account could have been given, but which were a daily grace if you lived with them; such as the art of being almost tragically impatient and yet making it as light as air; of being inexplicably sad and yet making it as clear as noon; of being unmistakably gay and yet making it as soft as dusk. Mrs Stringham by this time understood everything, was more than ever confirmed in wonder and admiration, in her view that it was life enough simply to feel her companion's feelings...   (Bk III ch. 1)

This uncertainty makes it teasingly difficult to know how to take the obviously important and symbolic scene in which Mrs

Stringham finds Milly sitting on the edge of a promontory high above an alpine valley and feels first, with alarm and horror, that Milly is wondering whether to jump, and then becomes convinced that Milly is, on the contrary, 'in a state of uplifted and unlimited possession':

She was looking down on the kingdoms of the earth, and though indeed that of itself might well go to the brain, it wouldn't be with a view of renouncing them. Was she choosing among them or did she want them all?   (Bk III ch. 1)

'All the kingdoms of the world, and the glory of them': it is not the last time that biblical echoes will attach themselves to Milly.

The conversation that follows Milly's return to the inn is teasing in a different way. In the course of a few pages James establishes that Milly has met Densher in New York, that he is important enough to her to cause her to be disingenuous about him, and that Mrs Stringham as a girl was at school in Switzerland with a Maud Manningham, now Maud Lowder, with whom she has since lost touch (indeed by whom she has since been 'shunted') but whom she would like to meet again now that she has 'at last something to show'. All this is shot through with Milly's puzzling and repeated assertions that she may not have much time before her, which possibility somehow has a bearing on her desire to travel directly to London. Milly's feyness distracts the reader, making it hard to notice how neatly James is smuggling a brace of coincidences into his novel. The chapter ends with Mrs Stringham sitting down to try to trace her former friend – 'there were connexions she remembered, addresses she could try' – and the next one begins with Milly seated at Mrs Lowder's dinner-table. The tragedy is now all wound up and ready to start.

Not, of course, that Milly, to whose consciousness we now for the first time have access, is aware that she is a character in a tragedy. She sees it rather as a fairy-tale, conjured up for her benefit by the admirable Mrs Stringham in the guise of fairy-godmother. We still cannot tell if this girl is really the princess the fairy-tale requires, but we quickly perceive that she is humble and guileless. She is overwhelmed by the kindness that she has instantly met with from Mrs Lowder on her arrival, in London, and innocently tells her neighbour at the dinner-table so:

It was as if she really cared for them, and it was magnificent fidelity – fidelity to Mrs Stringham, her own companion and Mrs Lowder's former schoolmate, the lady with the charming face and the rather high dress down there at the end.

Lord Mark took in through his nippers these balanced attributes of Susie. 'But isn't Mrs Stringham's fidelity then equally magnificent?'

'Well, it's a beautiful sentiment; but it isn't as if she had anything to *give*.'

'Hasn't she got you?' (Bk IV ch. 1)

It has not occurred to Milly to see herself as something to be snapped up. She immediately discounts the idea, and when Lord Mark tells her, 'Nobody here, you know, does anything for nothing', she knows that he is joking but fails to realize that the joke consists in telling her the truth.

Milly's 'success' with Mrs Lowder is made evident to the reader, if not to Milly herself, by the fact that she is seated next to Lord Mark. We have already encountered him as a rumour much discussed between Kate's sister Marian and the sisters of her dead husband, the odious Miss Condrips with their 'creeping curiosity', a rumour fiercely rejected by Kate herself. With his introduction to the reader in this scene the cast of the novel is almost complete (only two important supporting characters are still to be introduced) and the patterning out of which the plot will develop is at last plainly visible – the two young women, one poor and one rich, each the protégée of an older woman, one rich and one poor, and the two men, who at this stage in the novel both aspire to marry Kate, and between whom, we realize, as we survey Lord Mark through Milly's candid and observant eyes, there is a faint but alarming likeness:

It was difficult to guess his age – whether he were a young man who looked old or an old man who looked young; it seemed to prove nothing, as against other things, that he was bald and, as might have been said, slightly stale, or, more delicately perhaps, dry: there was such a fine little fidget of preoccupied life in him, and his eyes, at moments – though it was an appearance they could suddenly lose –

were as candid and clear as those of a pleasant boy. Very neat, very light, and so fair that there was little other indication of his moustache than his constantly feeling it – which was again boyish – he would have affected her as the most intellectual person present if he had not affected her as the most frivolous. (Bk IV ch. 1)

We feel disposed to like Densher, while it is hard not to see Lord Mark as both effete and slightly sinister, yet the similarity is there, and is apparent even to Milly, who chooses to see it as a national attribute:

Perhaps he was one of the cases she had heard of at home – those characteristic cases of people in England who concealed their play of mind so much more than they advertised it. Even Mr Densher a little did that. (Bk IV ch. 1)

We see too from this description of Lord Mark how shrewd a judge of character Milly can be, conscious though she is of the difficulties of decoding an alien culture previously known to her only, and patchily, from novels. This shrewdness makes us all the more certain that she has some strong motive for deceiving herself when, having discovered from Aunt Maud's confidences to Mrs Stringham and Marian's confidences to Milly herself that Densher is in love with Kate, she yet assures both herself and Mrs Stringham that Kate does not return his affection. Mrs Lowder has sworn her old friend to a partial silence – Densher must not be mentioned in front of Kate – and this has the effect of making Milly, in Kate's presence, unable to think of anything else. Kate has only to look or to smile at her for her to imagine the same look and smile being bestowed on Densher. This is all the more uncomfortable because she and Kate have rapidly become intimate friends; the intimacy is flawed a little by Milly's knowledge that Kate is keeping a secret from her, just as she is keeping one from Kate.

At this point the urbane and easy rhythm of Milly's London visit, a conventional round of shops and museums, is sharply broken by a moment and a vision of overwhelming intensity and authority. Like someone confronted by her *doppelgänger*, Milly is shown her own image, and the image tells her she must die. The scene begins deceptively, as key scenes in James's novels so often do, as a mixture of idyll and social comedy. Lord

Mark has arranged for Milly and her friends to be invited to a great country house – something, as everyone is being careful not to mention, that he has previously failed to do for Mrs Lowder and Kate alone. Again we see the pull and glamour of Milly's money. Lord Mark can open this particular social door for the wealthy but vulgar Mrs Lowder only by ushering the American princess through it ahead of her. (Milly's fortune too must have had its origin in trade, but it is saved from vulgarity by its exotic foreignness, by the romantic story of all the deaths that led to Milly acquiring it, and above all, unlike Mrs Lowder's substantial but all too calculable assets, by the sense that it is too vast to be counted.) We also begin to see that Lord Mark is definitely interested in Milly herself. It is he who precipitates the moment of vision.

'Have you seen the picture in the house, the beautiful one that's so like you?' – he was asking that as he stood before her; having come up at last with his smooth intimation that any wire he had pulled and yet wanted not to remind her of wasn't quite a reason for his having no joy at all. (Bk v ch. 2)

Milly, in her modesty, takes this for a social gambit, but she goes with him slowly through the gardens filled with people with 'lingering eyes' (are they staring at the legendary heiress or wondering why she looks so pale?) and into the rich-coloured labyrinth of the house:

The Bronzino was, it appeared, deep within, and the long afternoon light lingered for them on patches of old colour and waylaid them, as they went, in nooks and opening vistas. (Bk v ch. 2)

It is a scene that has happened before, but in reverse, in *The Portrait of a Lady* when Isabel, on her arrival at Gardencourt, insists on seeing the pictures and asks Ralph to show her the ghost:

'I might show it to you, but you'd never see it. The privilege isn't given to every one; it's not enviable. It has never been seen by a young, happy, innocent person like you. You must have suffered first, have suffered greatly, have gained some miserable knowledge. In that way your eyes are opened to it.' (ch. 5)

Milly's eyes are about to be opened. What she sees is both a climax and an end, 'a sort of magnificent maximum, the pink dawn of an apotheosis coming so curiously soon'. From this moment onwards everything will begin to change and fade and decay. It is the portrait, the Bronzino, which enforces this conviction, and the intensity of her recognition of it fills Milly's eyes with tears:

Perhaps it was her tears that made it just then so strange and fair – as wonderful as he had said : the face of a young woman, all splendidly drawn, down to the hands, and splendidly dressed; a face almost livid in hue, yet handsome in sadness and crowned with a mass of hair, rolled back and high, that must, before fading with time, have had a family resemblance to her own. The lady in question, at all events, with her slightly Michael-angelesque squareness, her eyes of other days, her full lips, her long neck, her recorded jewels, her brocaded and wasted reds, was a very great personage – only unaccompanied by a joy. And she was dead, dead, dead. Milly recognized her exactly in words that had nothing to do with her. 'I shall never be better than this.'   (Bk v ch. 2)

Ralph tells Isabel that he has seen the ghost 'long ago'; and when Isabel finally sees it too, the spirit that stands by her bedside like the true-lover's ghost in a ballad is the spirit of Ralph himself. Here Milly sees her own ghost, her 'pale sister', and James, that writer of ghost stories, enables her to do so without the need for any supernatural apparatus.

The lady in the portrait once really existed – she was called Lucrezia Panchiatichi, and Bronzino painted her in 1540 – but James is thinking here too of another woman, and one who was also 'dead, dead, dead'. Half a lifetime before he began work on *The Wings of the Dove*, James's cousin Minny Temple, a girl whose vivid and passionate love of life made her seem like a 'dancing flame of thought', died of tuberculosis in her early twenties. To James she had been

a young and shining apparition, a creature who owed to the charm of her every aspect (her aspects were so many!) and the originality, vivacity, audacity, generosity, of her spirit, an indescribable grace and weight – if one might impute weight to a being so imponderable in common scales.   (*Notes of a Son and Brother*, ch. 4)

The sense that her death gave him of a creature painfully

betrayed on the very threshold of life was one of the influences that led him to write *The Portrait of a Lady*. In that novel, though, he made the betrayal a willed and human one and took some of the pain out of Minny's death by transferring it to Ralph, the resigned and quizzical observer of others. In *The Wings of the Dove* he confronts the pain head-on. Minny's death is the dark seed from which the novel grows:

death, at the last, was dreadful to her; she would have given anything to live – and the image of this, which was long to remain with me, appeared so of the essence of tragedy that I was in the far-off after time to seek to lay the ghost by wrapping it, a particular occasion aiding, in the beauty and dignity of art.   (ch. 13)

But Milly too is to be subjected to willed and human betrayal, and even as she stands in front of the Bronzino that betrayal is beginning to draw near. Kate appears with a couple in tow, avid Lady Aldershaw and her shambling and half-witted husband, to whom she wants to display the amazing likeness that Lord Mark is showing to Milly herself. The scene dives briefly back into social comedy as the Aldershaws survey Milly and her double, Lady Aldershaw 'quite as if Milly had been the Bronzino and the Bronzino only Milly' and Lord Aldershaw with baffled blankness, and then resolves itself into pathos as the human pain and uncertainty of Milly's predicament becomes apparent at last. She is suddenly near to physical collapse, Lord Mark deftly whisks Lady Aldershaw away, cutting her off in mid-invitation, and Milly, left alone with Kate, asks her friend to give her 'the aid and comfort of her presence for a visit to Sir Luke Strett'. It is to consult this great doctor that Milly has come with such haste to London, and now she can put off the ordeal no longer. Her ostensible reason for asking for Kate's company is that she doesn't want Mrs Stringham 'to be worried if it's nothing. And to be still more worried – I mean before she need be – if it isn't.' Her hidden reason is to show a trust in Kate which will compensate for the silence that each is preserving towards the other over Merton Densher. And so, all unsuspecting, she puts a card into Kate's hand.

Sir Luke Strett is the first of the two supporting characters. He differs from the characters of the main plot in being impartial, scientific. He looks 'half like a general and half like a bishop' and sets before Milly a 'great empty cup of attention', surgically clean. However, like all Milly's relationships, this one too is determined by her money. Sir Luke charges a handsome fee. The first consultation ends with Kate, in the waiting-room, greeting Milly with 'such a face of sympathy as might have graced the vestibule of a dentist'. That false note reminds us of Milly's first impression of Kate, that 'with twenty other splendid qualities' she was 'the least bit brutal too'. '*She* would never in her life be ill', Milly is later to think. For the second consultation, Milly, having now 'shown Kate how she trusted her', comes alone.

The second consultation is the decisive one. Milly relates her family history 'with the easy habit of an interviewed heroine or a freak of nature at a show':

'When I was ten years old there were, with my father and my mother, six of us. I'm all that's left. But they died,' she went on, to be fair all round, 'of different things. Still, there it is.'   (Bk v ch. 3)

The black comedy of this reminds us of the wretched little river which drowned Kate's brother. It shows us too that if Milly sees herself as a heroine, it is as the heroine of a newspaper report, not of a romance. The great doctor urges her, indeed professionally advises her, to be happy, to be active, to live. Milly is not falsely reassured by this advice –

She had been treated – hadn't she – as if it were in her power to live; and yet one wasn't treated so – was one? – unless it had come up, quite as much, that one might die   (Bk v ch. 4)

but is roused by it to a state of excitement in which she sets off to wander alone through the streets of London, finding herself at last in Regent's Park, where she sits down exhausted:

Here were benches and smutty sheep; here were idle lads at games of ball, with their cries mild in the thick air; here were wanderers anxious and tired like herself; here doubtless were hundreds of others just in the same box. Their box, their great common anxiety, what was it, in this grim breathing-space, but the practical question of life?

They could live if they would; that is, like herself, they had been told so: she saw them all about her, on seats, digesting the information, recognizing it again as something in a slightly different shape familiar enough, the blessed old truth that they would live if they could.

(Bk v ch. 4)

Milly has now become an ordinary person, no longer a princess or a Bronzino lady but 'a poor girl – with her rent to pay for example – staring before her in a great city'.

The next evening the other, unsuspected half of her doom takes another step towards her. Mrs Lowder asks her to find out from Kate whether Merton Densher has returned to London, and Milly, reluctant to break the long silence on this subject between Kate and herself, inadvertently allows Mrs Lowder to guess the true nature of her feelings for Densher. In fact she doesn't need to ask Mrs Lowder's question. Kate is evidently in a keyed-up state – Milly feels, almost in fear, that she is 'alone with a creature who paced like a panther' – and she speaks strangely, warning Milly that she would be wiser to 'drop' her aunt and herself. 'We're of no use to you – it's decent to tell you. You'd be of use to us, but that's a different matter.' When Milly demands in bewilderment, 'Why do you say such things to me?' Kate embraces her with the words, 'Because you're a dove.' Milly has just lost one identity. She seizes on this replacement with a strange sense of relief. From now on she will be a dove, and she must study to discover what her new rôle will entail.

Densher, meanwhile, as Milly has guessed, has indeed returned to London. He has returned with the firm intention of putting an end to the frustrating game that he and Kate have been playing, an intention that is weakened by his first encounter with Kate at Euston Station and more or less destroyed when, on their second attempt at a rendezvous, in the National Gallery, they unexpectedly run into little Miss Theale, the American girl he met in New York, who invites the pair of them back to lunch at her hotel. In effect there is a trial of strength between Densher and Kate, and it is Densher who loses. Kate sees no reason to abandon their previous plan, and, she tells him, she now has a new one, a mysterious new plan

which somehow involves Milly and which, by a combination of
will-power and embraces, she forces Densher to assent to.

Kate has a plan, perhaps not quite fully formed as yet but
growing steadily in the dark places of her mind, and Densher
is the necessary tool. To trap Milly she must first trap Densher,
and in this she has three accomplices, Mrs Lowder, Mrs
Stringham and Milly herself.

Mrs Stringham, grief-stricken by what she has learnt at the
encounter with Sir Luke Strett that Milly has contrived for her,
rushes round to confide in her old friend. Mrs Lowder refuses
to join her in grieving for Milly – 'I might be crying now', she
plumply remarks, 'if I weren't writing letters' – but is perfectly
willing to scheme for her. The doctor has told Mrs Stringham
that Milly must be made happy, and happiness for Milly would
be marriage to Merton Densher. It is this that the two older
women must arrange. Even when Mrs Lowder lets slip a fact
she has hitherto concealed, that Kate returns Densher's
affection, Mrs Stringham, in her desperation, is not checked.
'Kate wasn't in danger, Kate wasn't pathetic; Kate Croy,
whatever happened, would take care of Kate Croy.'

Mrs Lowder enters into the plot with mixed feelings. She had
wanted Milly to make a 'great' marriage – not for Milly's sake,
of course, but for Kate's. 'I saw your girl – I don't mind telling
you – helping my girl', she tells Mrs Stringham. However this
new plan, if it comes off, will have the advantage of disposing
of Densher, of whom she is more afraid than she likes to admit.
She has already, in fact, taken steps to persuade Milly that
Kate doesn't care for Densher, and quickly makes an
opportunity to inform Densher himself that she has done so:

'I'm treating you handsomely, I'm looking after it for you. I *can* – I
can smooth your path. She's charming, she's clever and she's good.
And her fortune's a real fortune.'   (Bk vi ch. 4)

Densher, at this stage, feels able to reply with sarcasm to her
attempt to buy him off with Milly's money. He has not yet
realized what the 'beauty' of Kate's plan consists of.

As for Milly herself, she makes the whole plan possible by her
own readiness, her desperate need, to believe that Densher's
love for Kate is unrequited. This readiness makes her eager to

overlook the evidence to the contrary – why should Kate have
kept so silent about a lover she *didn't* care for; why should she
wear so visibly the signs of his return, make occasion to meet
him in the National Gallery? Like Isabel, Milly chooses to be
deceived; but unlike Isabel, trapped by her false friend but
warned by her true one, Milly is surrounded by a conspiracy of
encouragement and assistance in her delusion from true and
false friends alike, while Ralph, that quizzical observer, has
mutated, by way of Maisie's Sir Claude, into vague and idle
Densher himself. Christ warned the apostles that to survive in
a dangerous world they must be 'wise as serpents and harmless
as doves'. Milly has only the wisdom of a dove, while Kate,
who has tasted the fruit of the tree and is now busily inducing
Densher to eat, has acquired the guile and cunning of the
snake. And for Milly, unlike the flourishing Isabel, the sands
are running out. No wonder that, as they sink in the glass, she
grasps hold of anything, anything at all, that will give her a
taste of life before it is too late.

Kate has guile and cunning, but she also has luck. The first
steps of the plot involve persuading Densher that what she is
asking him to do is only what he would have done anyway:
going to see Milly, treating her with ordinary friendliness.
Then, just at the point when he feels he is getting in too deep
and is nervously wondering about the possibilities of retreat,
Kate appears and offers to rescue him by telling Milly the
truth:

'It will of course greatly upset her. But you needn't trouble about
that. She won't die of it.'   (Bk vi ch. 5)

She has managed to strike at the psychological moment. The
point at which it is too early to need to resist temptation has
been deftly turned into the point at which it is too late even to
try. Densher, persuading himself as hard as he can that he is
doing the 'decent' thing, continues along Kate's road, and still
he can't allow himself to see where that road is leading.

Kate herself, as she shoves and coaxes Densher further down
the road, is curiously untroubled by feelings of guilt or doubt:

It may be declared for Kate, at all events, that her sincerity about her
friend, through this time, was deep, her compassionate imagination

strong; and that these things gave her a virtue, a good conscience, a credibility for herself, so to speak, that were later to be precious to her.   (Bk VII ch. 3)

The beauty of her plan, as she sees it, is that it will be equally beneficial to everyone. The American princess has turned out to be a beggar-maid in disguise, all her fabulous wealth useless to her since it is unable to ransom her from impending death. 'I shouldn't care for her if she hadn't so much', Kate tells Densher:

And then as it made him laugh not quite happily: 'I shouldn't trouble about her if there were one thing she did have ... She has nothing.'   (Bk VI ch. 4)

How kind, then, of Kate to lend to her best friend, since given Milly's state of health it *can* only be a loan, the one thing that will make her last months happy, and how appropriate that Kate will acquire in return the very freedom she has envied Milly so much, the freedom of money. Even Aunt Maud and Mrs Stringham will be happy. A perfectly beautiful plan, as long as she can pull it off. The weak link, of course, is Densher. 'Infirm of purpose! Give me the daggers', said Lady Macbeth to her quailing husband, but the point is going to come when Kate will have to leave Densher to act unaided. Confident of her power over him, Kate is sure that he will be an effective ally, an obedient tool, provided she doesn't tell him too much too soon.

In this way the girl who a few months earlier had winced at her sister's obsession with Mrs Lowder's money, reflecting to herself 'how poor you might become when you minded so much the absence of wealth', brings herself to the point of betraying her best friend and acting as procuress to her own lover. She doesn't notice what has happened to her or how the nature of her relationship with Densher is changing under the pressure of her plan. She feels strong, justified, in control.

The scene now changes to Venice, the city where James wrote part of *The Portrait of a Lady* and which he connected so strongly with that novel that he began the preface to *Portrait* in the New York edition with an evocation of it. Milly has travelled south for her health, and of course her devoted London friends and her even more devoted Boston one have travelled with her. At another level, Milly has chosen to defy death by dying in a palace, thus at last really living the rôle of princess. Palaces are easy to come by in Venice where every large house is a *palazzo*. Milly, in those moments of humble exhaustion in Regent's Park, had seen herself as a poor girl with her rent to get – Palazzo Leporelli is a rented palace, found for her by the second of the supporting characters, Sir Luke's opposite and antitype, Eugenio the perfect major-domo. When we first encounter her there she is enjoying its cool gothic and baroque magnificence alone, with a sensation of hovering in her high upper rooms above the Grand Canal which is almost the feeling of freedom, although these are rooms she is never to leave again.

Her trance of solitary possession is broken by the entrance of Lord Mark. That disturbing likeness between Lord Mark and Densher that we noticed earlier suddenly becomes vivid as we discover the purpose of his visit: he has come to propose to Milly, and it is not the girl but the money that is his object. Milly, so easily deceived by Densher, has no difficulty in seeing through Lord Mark, and the ugliness of what she sees transfers itself in the reader's mind to the man Milly is unable to distrust:

For a man in whom the vision of her money should be intense, in whom it should be most of the ground for 'making up' to her, any prospective failure on her part to be long for this world might easily count as a positive attraction. Such a man, proposing to please, persuade, secure her, appropriate her for such a time, shorter or longer, as nature and the doctors should allow, would make the best of her, ill, damaged, disagreeable though she might be, for the sake of eventual benefits... (Bk VII ch. 4)

Lord Mark's attempt at a declaration of passion fails so completely to ring true that Milly laughs, and Lord Mark 'intelligently, helplessly, almost comically' accepts defeat – for the moment. However, when Milly tries to remind him of his commitment to Kate he tells her, as something she must know already, that Kate is 'very much in love with a particular person'. Milly's confident denial of this – she 'quite flushed at having so crude a blunder imputed to her' – is followed by the entrance of a servant announcing another visitor. Merton Densher has now arrived in Venice.

At this point, though the first-time reader has no way of knowing it, Milly quietly bows out of her own novel. From now on we will see her, indeed we will see everything, only through Densher's eyes. It is a bold move on James's part (though some critics take it for a timid one, as if James were retreating on tiptoe from Milly's deathbed) and its effect is to force us into appalled complicity with Densher as he squirms on the hook of his predicament. We become Densher – there is no one else left for us to be. But in the economy of a well-made novel nothing is used for one purpose only, and this device has several other functions. It preserves both the loneliness of Milly's ordeal and the mystery of her personality, and in the final stages of the novel it becomes essential to the plot. Just as, in real life, when we try to imagine the thoughts and sensations of the dying, we come painfully up against the limits of our own imaginations, so we relive the experience inside the novel as we see Densher's imagination fail to encompass Milly's suffering. Milly is tested to destruction and we are left not knowing the outcome of the test. To Mrs Stringham she is a princess, to Lord Mark she is a Bronzino, to Kate she is a dove, to herself she is an ordinary girl or at worst an ordinary heroine. To the reader she remains a mystery, a white space that may be full of unimaginable marvels or may simply be empty.

Densher, on his arrival in Venice, is more preoccupied with Kate than with Milly. He has never been a believer in Milly's cult, partly because, ironically, the glamour of money has very little power over him. He has never really seen why Kate should not marry him just as he is, but now, when he proposes yet again this simple solution to their dilemma, she says sharply, 'Do you want to kill her? We've told too many lies.' Densher believes himself not to have told any, but he feels angry and humiliated at his own submission to Kate's plan. Significantly, it is the submission that humiliates him, not the nature of the plan itself:

He held his breath a little as it came home to him with supreme sharpness that, whereas he had done absolutely everything that Kate had wanted, she had done nothing whatever that he had.

(Bk VIII ch. 1)

Resentfully he decides to impose his own will on Kate. If she will submit to him physically he will tell any lie she wants. Kate accepts his offer, trapping Densher with his own blackmail. She will pay for his services in advance and then he will have no choice.

Now at last the plan can be put into words between them. This conversation takes place, horribly, at an evening party at Palazzo Leporelli with Milly, radiantly sacrificial in a white dress, smiling at them from across the room. It begins with Kate drawing Densher's attention to Milly's pearls:

'She's a dove, and one somehow doesn't think of doves as bejewelled. Yet they suit her down to the ground.'
　'Yes – down to the ground is the word.'

Down to the ground, where Milly so soon will go.

'Pearls have such a magic that they suit every one.'
　'They would uncommonly suit you.'
　'Oh yes, I see myself!'

She sees herself, and Densher sees her too, in the only pearls he has any chance of giving her, Milly's pearls. And so, slowly, carefully, deviously they come to the point.

'Since she's to die I'm to marry her?'
　'To marry her.'
　'So that when her death has taken place I shall in the natural course have money?'
　'You'll in the natural course have money. We shall in the natural course be free.'
(Bk VIII ch. 3)

In the name of that freedom each confines the other. Kate comes to Densher's rooms as she has promised and then returns to England with Mrs Lowder, leaving Densher to put the plan into action.

As a conspirator Densher is a pathetic failure. Obsessed by the physical memory of Kate, cringing at his own ignominious rôle, for three weeks he manages to persuade himself that the right course of action is to do nothing; and at the end of three weeks, on the day of the first winter storm, his punishment begins. Calling as usual at the palace, he is refused admittance. The ladies, it seems, are 'a "leetle" fatigued, just a "leetle leetle", and without any cause named for it'. Densher retreats into the driving rain under the courteously contemptuous eyes of Eugenio who has always known, and shows it, that Densher is after Milly's money, 'an opinion of him that there was no attacking, no disproving, no (what was worst of all) even noticing'. Too restless to return to his rooms, he makes his way to the Piazza San Marco. The great square, invaded by the storm, is like an image of the destruction of civilization, 'the drawing-room of Europe, profaned and bewildered by some reverse of fortune'. Making his way round the crowded arcades, Densher is suddenly arrested by a face behind the glass of a café window. Kate, in her father's sordid little room, saw her own face in the mirror; Milly confronted herself and her own mortality in the Bronzino; and now Densher too faces his own image. His double eyes him indifferently, with dawning recognition but without a greeting, and then turns back to his contemplation of the wall. It is Lord Mark, and his presence explains everything:

The weather had changed, the rain was ugly, the wind wicked, the sea impossible, *because* of Lord Mark. It was because of him, *a fortiori*, that the palace was closed.   (Bk IX ch. 2)

The truth of this is confirmed three days later when Mrs Stringham arrives at Densher's lodgings, ravaged by rain and tears, and tells him, in an image whose despair is the sharp corollary of the failed calculation expressed by Lord Mark's vacant stare, that Milly 'has turned her face to the wall'. Lord Mark, unsuccessfully reopening his courtship of Kate, has worked out the grounds for her rejection of him, and he has now presented Milly with the result of his deductions in a last attempt to win her instead. Mrs Stringham has come to beg the shrinking Densher to deny to Milly, as the only hope of saving her, this slander which they both know to be the truth. This section of the novel ends with Densher being gravely informed by Sir Luke that Milly would like to see him; and then, unexpectedly, we find ourselves, with Densher, back in London, the dying Milly left behind in her Venetian solitude. Now at last the title of the novel takes on its full meaning in the terrible words of the psalmist:

My heart is sore pained within me: and the terrors of death are fallen upon me. Fearfulness and trembling are come upon me, and horror hath overwhelmed me. And I said, Oh that I had wings like a dove! for then would I fly away, and be at rest. Lo, then would I wander far off, and remain in the wilderness. I would hasten my escape from the windy storm and tempest. Destroy, O Lord, and divide their tongues: for I have seen violence and strife in the city. Day and night they go about it upon the walls thereof: mischief also and sorrow are in the midst of it. Wickedness is in the midst thereof: deceit and guile depart not from her streets. For it was not an enemy that reproached me; then I could have borne it: neither was it he that hated me that did magnify himself against me; then I would have hid myself from him: but it was thou, a man mine equal, my guide, and mine acquaintance. (Psalm 55)

But while Milly faces death in the light of that appalling knowledge, we are not there. We are in the Lancaster Gate drawing-room, watching Densher sinking into the embrace of Aunt Maud's sympathy, as cosily enveloping as a plush sofa.

For this is a novel concerned ultimately not with the victim but with the betrayers. Where Gilbert Osmond, like George Eliot's Grandcourt, was invulnerable in the hard shell of his egotism, Densher suffers, though the ground of his suffering is not the damage he has done to Milly but the damage he has done to his own idea of himself. It is in order not to think about the damage he has done to Milly, still living, still in pain, that he frequents the house in Lancaster Gate where Mrs Lowder, enjoying her privileged view of the tragedy 'very much as a stout citizen's wife might have sat, during a play that made people cry, in the pit or the family-circle', is only too eager to help him to talk about Milly in the past tense.

The triangular situation which now obtains, with Mrs Lowder avidly pouring tea for Densher while Kate effaces herself, is a parodic version of the beginning of the novel, and Densher is aware of this. Overwhelmed by the need to escape from the sick taste of what he has become, he resolves to push things further back still. He arranges to walk in the park with Kate as in the first days of their courtship, though now under winter trees, and there begs her to cancel out the nightmare by marrying him.

'We've played our dreadful game, and we've lost. We owe it to ourselves, we owe it to our feeling *for* ourselves and for each other, not to wait another day. Our marriage will – fundamentally, somehow, don't you see? – right everything that's wrong ... we shall only wonder at our past fear. It will seem an ugly madness. It will seem a bad dream.   (Bk x ch. 2)

Kate, however, seems to feel that the game is neither lost nor over. She has already presented Densher with her own version of what they have done to, or as she prefers to see it, for Milly, a bland and polished and painless version in which Milly is dying satisfied to have 'realized her passion'; now she greets his proposal with a cryptic partial assent.

'Of course, if it's that you really *know* something ?'

If he really *knows* something she will marry him, but Densher at first doesn't even know what she is talking about. Then suddenly he does know, and the realization makes him redden with shame and with something that is almost horror at Kate's cool calculation of possibilities. The game is not yet over, and he can't prevent Kate from playing it to the end.

   The first-time reader is left puzzled as to what it is that Densher might really know, though seeing clearly enough the widening gulf between two people no longer talking the same moral language. James, far from explaining matters, teasingly draws out the suspense in the following chapter in which something happens to Densher on Christmas Eve, something that answers Kate's question, something that keeps him awake all night and sends him out early into the foggy air of Christmas morning. He is going to see Kate, but he makes his way first to Sir Luke Strett's house where he finds a carriage waiting outside. It is Mrs Lowder's brougham, and as he draws nearer to it he is ambushed by an image from that day of storm in Venice. Looking from the window, where he had expected to see Kate, is the face of his rival Lord Mark. He is still digesting the shock of this when Mrs Lowder comes out of the doctor's house and tells him, in a snatch of dialogue that is pure black comedy, that Milly is dead:

'Our dear dove then, as Kate calls her, has folded her wonderful wings.'   (Bk x ch. 3)

As Mrs Lowder embroiders this theme, Densher can only woodenly repeat a fragment of each thing she says, while she takes his embarrassment for mourning decently controlled. She tells him, too, that Kate is spending Christmas 'in the bosom of her more immediate family', and Densher accordingly calls at Mrs Condrip's little house in Chelsea.

We are back in the sordid little room in which the novel began, and Kate's father is lying in bed upstairs, crying in terror 'of somebody – of something'. It is in the sordid little room, escape from which has motivated all Kate's actions, that Densher confronts her with the success of her plan. Densher has received a letter from Milly, written while she was still able to write and kept to be sent as a Christmas gift. He has brought it to Kate unopened, but there is no doubt about what it contains. Kate has guessed right after all and Milly has left him a fortune. To Densher this letter is something infinitely precious which he has brought to Kate as a pledge of his feeling for her; to Kate his action is simply a proof of Milly's growing power over him. Earlier, in the grip of her plan, she had believed herself proof against jealousy; now she feels insidiously threatened by a dead girl. Kate is her father's daughter – like him, she has done an 'impossible' thing – but she has hardened herself early against tears and terror. She takes Densher's pledge and throws it in the fire, and together they watch it burn.

It is in this final section of the novel that James confronts us with the moral riddle that *The Portrait of a Lady* failed to ask. It was easy to feel pity as Madame Merle wailed, 'Have I been so vile all for nothing?' and to shrink from the cold sadism of Osmond, but here nothing is easy. Milly, whether heroine or victim, has vanished into darkness, and we are left with a choice

between the ruthless directness of Kate, honest in its own terms
and still certain of its objective, and the moral squeamishness of
the manipulated Densher, no longer able to anaesthetize his
raw imagination against the pain of the destruction he has
brought about. Which do we most resemble? Which would it
be more terrible to be? What is certain is that the dreadful
game they have played has required both of them. The
symbiotic relationship which began as love has brought them
to this end.

For both of them now it is a time of waiting. Kate waits for
the material reward of all her planning, the lawyer's letter from
New York. Densher waits for an immaterial thing. Just as
earlier, in Venice, he had been haunted by the physical
memory of Kate's lovemaking, so now he is haunted by Milly's
letter. While Milly still lived he had tried to turn his thoughts
away. 'Knowingly to hang about in London while the pain
went on – what would that do but make his days impossible?'
Now he strains his imagination to capture what he has
irrevocably lost:

He took to himself at such hours ... that he should never, never know
what had been in Milly's letter. The intention announced in it he
should but too probably know; only that would have been, but for the
depths of his spirit, the least part of it. The part of it missed for ever
was the turn she would have given her act. This turn had possibilities
that, somehow, by wondering about them, his imagination had
extraordinarily filled out and refined. It had made of them a
revelation the loss of which was like the sight of a priceless pearl cast
before his eyes – his pledge given not to save it – into the fathomless
sea, or rather even it was like the sacrifice of something sentient and
throbbing, something that, for the spiritual ear, might have been
audible as a faint far wail.   (Bk x ch. 6)

The 'long, priceless chain' of the necklace that Kate coveted so
has become a single lost pearl whose matchless beauty Densher
alone can see. He feels like Othello, who 'like the base Indian,
threw a pearl away / Richer than all his tribe', but while
Othello knew that the 'priceless pearl' that he had destroyed
and lost was Desdemona herself, Densher mourns and longs not
for Milly but for the letter. That 'faint far wail' to which he
listens so intently as he waits for the sounds of the world to stifle

it is still more bearable than the agonized silence in which Milly
lay with her face to the wall. Yet at the same time it *is* Milly,
and as we strain our ears to catch it too we will never know
whether this last echo of her is really only the wailing of
Densher's stricken conscience sounding faintly in his inner ear.

For two months Kate and Densher wait, and pretend to each
other that they are now free as never before to enjoy each
other's company, and find excuses not to exercise that freedom.
The need that Densher feels 'to bury in the dark blindness of
each other's arms the knowledge of each other that they
couldn't undo' is acted out in a bland avoidance of any
mention of what now lies between them. When the lawyer's
letter arrives he sends it to Kate unopened. He has come to a
decision that he hopes she will sense and honour without words.
Together they will repudiate the money, and he will return the
envelope, still unopened, to New York. But when Kate arrives
in his rooms she has already opened and read the letter.
Cheated of his fine moral gesture, Densher has all the same
reached the point where he can be manipulated no further, and
Kate realizes this. She lucidly expresses to him the ultimatum
he is now presenting her with:

'You'll marry me without the money; you won't marry me with it.
If I don't consent *you* don't.'   (Bk x ch. 6)

Densher, thinking he is clarifying her choice, tells her that if she
loses him she will lose nothing else. He will give her the money.

It is now that the novel presents us with its final twist. Kate
has plotted and lied and betrayed for that money, and now,
with the solid rewards of her plan before her, she faces total
defeat. Yet her choice now, she tells Densher, depends on
something quite different:

'Your word of honour that you're not in love with her memory.'

This is no longer jealousy, it is clear vision, though Densher
tries to brush away with a sighing word what he cannot deny:

'Oh – her memory!'
  'Ah' – She made a high gesture – 'don't speak of it as if you
couldn't be. *I* could in your place; and you're one for whom it will do.
Her memory's your love. You *want* no other.'

There is nothing left for either of them now but honesty. For Densher, that means the reassertion of his promise, but Kate knows now, and moves with clarity towards the only possible end. They have killed the love between them, and Densher, listening so intently to that 'faint far wail', has not even noticed it die.

He heard her out in stillness, watching her face but not moving. Then he only said: 'I'll marry you, mind you, in an hour.'
  'As we were?'
  'As we were.'
  But she turned to the door, and her headshake was now the end. 'We shall never be again as we were!'

CHAPTER 8

The Golden Bowl

The Golden Bowl, James's last completed novel, presents the reader with a paradox; it is the culmination of his life's work and only James could have written it, and yet it is curiously unlike anything that preceded it. Like Shakespeare's *Tempest*, which it in some ways resembles, it insists on being read as a final work, and like *The Tempest* it is concerned with treachery and forgiveness – but, despite the Shakespearian echoes, James is fundamentally dealing with far more ancient material. For all its slow unfolding – not so much leisurely as suspense-building – his plot has all the tightness, balance and inevitability of a Greek tragedy. We have to conflate these two dramatic analogies and imagine Maggie Verver as a Miranda in the predicament of Medea to realize the full complexity of James's theme. But Charlotte too is Medea; like a palindrome, the novel can be read in both directions, and either way it provides us with a riddle and a mystery, something that we must solve and something that in the end we can only wonder at.

James's novels tend to start deceptively. In the opening chapters of *The Golden Bowl* we are given a deceptive likeness to his previous novel. As in *The Wings of the Dove*, the plot centres on an American princess, but where Milly's title was only a poetic way of expressing the crude fact that she had money, in Maggie Verver's case money has bought her a real prince. We have already encountered, in James's earlier novels, the silly or falsely shrewd American woman who marries for the sake of a meaningless European title. Here it is different. Adam Verver, Maggie's millionaire father, is an art collector, and the Prince has been carefully authenticated. He is 'a rarity, an object of beauty, an object of price', and there is no doubt about his provenance; 'the follies and the crimes, the plunder and the waste' of his ancestors have all been documented, right back to the 'infamous Pope' who founded his line. Even the dubious-seeming family connection with Amerigo Vespucci, which so much increases his heritage value for the Ververs, is 'perfectly historic'. There has to be a flaw of course – real princes do not marry the naïve little daughters of retired industrialists for nothing, or even for love – but the Ververs imagine that they have taken this into consideration. Adam Verver is as able to make up for the Prince's financial deficiencies as Maggie is to believe in his disinterestedness despite them. She expresses her trust in him in a spoilt little rich girl image drawn from her experience of luxury liners:

'Why it's the best cabin and the main deck and the engine-room and the steward's pantry! It's the ship itself – it's the whole line. It's the captain's table and all one's luggage – one's reading for the trip.'

(Bk I ch. I)

This extended metaphor forms part of a series of ship images at the start of the novel that leads into the sea imagery which is to be a major symbolic pattern later in the book. Maggie, in her ingenuous comparison of her father's art collecting to the amassing of pirate hoards, makes the significant point, 'we've had extraordinary luck – we've never lost anything yet'. The Prince asks Mrs Assingham, who has arranged his approaching marriage, to continue to pilot him through the voyage ahead 'across the unknown sea', only to be told that on the contrary he is 'practically *in* port. The port of the Golden Isles.' These images are introduced casually by James and could be dismissed by the reader at this stage as mere passing figures of speech. More striking and ominous is the recollection by the Prince of a literary image encountered in childhood:

He remembered to have read as a boy a wonderful tale by Allan Poe, his prospective wife's countryman – which was a thing to show, by the way, what imagination Americans *could* have: the story of the shipwrecked Gordon Pym, who, drifting in a small boat further toward the North Pole – or was it the South? – than anyone had ever done, found at a given moment before him a thickness of white air that was like a dazzling curtain of light, concealing as darkness conceals, yet of the colour of milk or of snow. (Bk I ch. 1)

Poe's curious story, part hoaxing tall tale, part fable of white supremacy written to reinforce the racist fantasies of the slave-owning Southern society that Miss Birdseye spent her life opposing, was simply a source of potent dream-images for the young Amerigo who, polyglot child that he was, could even have read it in Baudelaire's translation. James not only brilliantly captures the way in which children do read such books – *Gulliver's Travels*, *Robinson Crusoe*, *King Solomon's Mines* – not for their social content but for their archetypal motifs, but also implies that to the boy Amerigo the continent to which his ancestor gave its name was a place as alluring and mysterious as Europe is for the Ververs. The summoning up by the adult Amerigo of this magical image of 'a thickness of white air' to crystallize his faint unease at the cultural gap between himself and 'his new friends' is our first hint that the novel will contain tempest, shipwreck, sea change and rough magic.

At this early stage of the novel, though, the dominant image is money. We first meet the Prince among the spoils of Bond Street – 'objects massive and lumpish, in silver and gold' – at the moment when his six months' pursuit has just been rewarded with capture. That afternoon he has become engaged, not to Maggie but to her fortune:

He was to dine at half-past eight o'clock with the young lady on whose behalf, and on whose father's, the London lawyers had reached an inspired harmony with his own man of business. (Bk I ch. 1)

At this stage his idea of his young bride is not very different from Colonel Assingham's:

'She's very nice, but she always seems to me more than anything else the young woman who has a million a year.' (Bk I ch. 4)

Though he thinks her charming and is aware of her innocence and imagination, he is principally concerned with the fact that he has a future to make and that 'the material for the making had to be Mr Verver's millions'.

Mrs Assingham's mention of the Golden Isles rouses another

Shakespearian echo – the fortune-hunting Bassanio in *The Merchant of Venice* describing another millionaire's daughter:

> her sunny locks
> Hang on her temples like a golden fleece,
> Which makes her seat of Belmont Colchis' strand,
> And many Jasons come in quest of her.
>
> (Act 1 Sc. 1)

Jason's involvement with the woman he meets on Colchis' strand will be central to the novel and, as if that faint echo has summoned her up, the first of her avatars unexpectedly makes its appearance. The Prince's former relationship with Charlotte Stant is, of course, the hidden flaw that the Ververs have failed to spot, and his frankly physical appraisal of her now, so different from his languid thoughts about Maggie, provides the nearest thing to an erotic moment that we have yet encountered in any James novel – until, that is, its disquieting conclusion:

> He saw again that her thick hair was, vulgarly speaking, brown, but that there was a shade of tawny autumn leaf in it for 'appreciation' – a colour indescribable and of which he had known no other case, something that gave her at moments the sylvan head of a huntress. He saw the sleeves of her jacket drawn to her wrists, but he again made out the free arms within them to be of the completely rounded, the polished slimness that Florentine sculptors in the great time had loved and of which the apparent firmness is expressed in their old silver and old bronze. He knew her narrow hands, he knew her long fingers and the shape and colour of her finger-nails, he knew her special beauty of movement and line when she turned her back, and the perfect working of all her main attachments, that of some wonderful finished instrument, something intently made for exhibition, for a prize. He knew above all the extraordinary fineness of her flexible waist, the stem of an expanded flower, which gave her a likeness also to some long, loose silk purse, well filled with gold-pieces, but having been passed empty through a finger-ring that held it together.
>
> (Bk 1 ch. 3)

This is the picture of a man looking at a woman he finds sexually compelling, a woman, as the evocation of her bare arms under her jacket powerfully suggests, that he has almost certainly seen naked, and yet the run of the images, Greek goddess, art object, treasure, precision instrument, prize, ends up, as if inevitably, with that purse of gold coins. To clinch it, we see him sensuously experiencing in imagination not the woman but the gold:

It was as if, before she turned to him, he had weighed the whole thing in his open palm and even heard a little the chink of the metal.

Charlotte is to dominate the first half of the novel, and this scene shows the Prince reflecting not only on her physical beauty but also on her remarkable intelligence and strength of mind which are implicitly contrasted with Maggie's innocence and naïvely romantic imagination. Intelligence, in fact, is to be an important theme in the novel. The Prince himself, we learn in the opening pages, is convinced that he is not 'frivolous or stupid', but when Mrs Assingham teasingly calls him 'Machiavelli' he rather ruefully replies, 'I wish indeed I had his genius.' We are to discover that although he excels in all the skills necessary for the demanding life style of aristocratic leisure, 'in shooting, in riding, in golfing, in walking, over the fine diagonals of meadow-paths or round the pocketed corners of billiard tables', he is damagingly incapable of rapid or decisive thought.

As for the Ververs themselves, in the early part of the book it is easy to underestimate them – in fact James takes pains to make sure that we do. It is only in the second half of the novel that we get inside Maggie's mind and begin to understand its extraordinary workings. At the outset, all we have to go on is Mrs Assingham's curious assertion 'She wasn't born to know evil. She must never know it', and it is hard for us to know to what extent this describes Maggie's Miranda-like condition, brought up, as she has been, alone with her father on a desert island of money, and to what extent it merely represents Mrs Assingham's self-justification for having concealed from Maggie the Prince's former liaison with her best friend. In judging Adam Verver we are misled by the absurdity of his belief that it is possible to be a self-taught expert in all the fine and applied arts, an unerring and instinctive judge of 'representative precious objects, great ancient pictures and other works of art, fine eminent "pieces" in gold, in silver, in enamel, majolica, ivory, bronze'; a belief only less absurd than that of the inhabitants of American City that a great art gallery, a 'museum of museums', can be filled with treasures as hastily as it can be built. In fact, of course, Adam Verver's collection is less a pirate's hoard than a dragon's, and the amassing of it is a loving, patient, ruthless manifestation of greed. His love of the beautiful can only be consummated by acquisition. He too has reached the Golden Isles and now he is busy 'rifling' them. The quality of his connoisseurship is summed up by his purchase of the Prince, the flawed art object that he mistakes for a 'perfect crystal'. The quality of his power is something that we will not appreciate until the end of the novel. Superficially – lacking, as he does, the cultural trappings which make wealth appear imposing – he seems a meek and compliant little man, Andrew Carnegie played by Charlie Chaplin.

However, where in an earlier James novel the complex of forces created by these four diverse intelligences would determine the outcome of the story, here there are larger and darker powers at work. It only needs a single human action to bring them into play, and that action is Charlotte's. On the pretext of looking for a wedding present for Maggie she persuades the Prince to spend a few clandestine hours with her, hours which, like the gift she plans to offer him, will be 'a small ricordo', an ineffaceable little memory of intimacy and deception on the very eve of his marriage. Their search leads them to the golden bowl, and from that point on the action of the novel is inevitable. A golden bowl is always a powerful symbol. In Ecclesiastes – 'or ever the silver cord be loosed, or the golden bowl be broken' – it is a figure of death, while Blake's

> Can Wisdom be put in a silver rod?
> Or Love in a golden bowl?
>
> *(The Book of Thel)*

mocks the powerlessness of the anxious, controlling human mind. However, here the gilded, flawed, doom-laden crystal goblet is not just the central image of the novel, it is an agent of the plot as powerful and magical as the demonic wishing-bottle in Robert Louis Stevenson's haunting story 'The Bottle Imp':

He opened a lock-fast place, and took out a round-bellied bottle with a long neck; the glass of it was white like milk, with changing rainbow colours in the grain. Withinsides something obscurely moved, like a shadow and a fire.

Like Stevenson's bottle, the bowl is beautiful, alarming and unlucky – 'it seemed indeed to warn off the prudent admirer' – and like the bottle it knows and sticks to its victims; but whereas anyone who was rash enough could purchase the bottle, the little Bloomsbury shopman prefers to sell his wares 'to right people'. Though the Prince tries nervously to repudiate it – 'Per Dio I'm superstitious! A crack's a crack – and an omen's an omen' – his attempt to escape from the bowl in fact ensures the devastating way in which it will return into his life.

The bowl is an agent of the plot, but it is not a mere plot contrivance. Like the Bronzino portrait which shows Milly Theale her own ghost, James uses it to create a supernatural effect through natural means, but here the magic is all-embracing and all-consuming. While London and Venice exist despite Milly's life or death, just as Paris and its environs continue unchanged after Strether has returned to Woollett, in *The Golden Bowl*, once the spell is wound up and the tragedy set in motion, there is no longer any outside world. All the novel's many houses are in fact only one house, 'the great black house' where the Prince and Charlotte look down from the balcony, as if from 'the peopled battlements of a castle', at Maggie and her father returning from the park with the Principino. This self-containment of the action, which has troubled many critics, is essential to the impact and meaning of the novel. To understand this we have only to think of the great house in which a Greek tragedy unfolds, or of Prospero's 'bare island'.

However, the Ververs too have their part to play in initiating the tragic action. The Prince marries Maggie in order to have the power to shape his own life, the power of her father's money, but in fact the marriage simply turns him into a handsome stud-animal, while the child which owes both its title and its beauty to his paternity becomes an additional bond between Maggie and her father. Maggie herself is troubled by this – the death of her mother had turned her, at ten years old, into her father's 'wife', and now, physically in love with her husband but psychologically still tied to her father, she needs to free herself from this rôle – but her proposal of Charlotte as substitute daughter–wife is unthinkingly exploitative, even if also unwittingly so. Contained as she still is within the circle of her father's personality, Maggie is unable to see him objectively, while the comic threat of Mrs Rance and the Miss Lutches, those predatory female vultures, suggests to her that he is still an attractive man. Like Strether with poor little Jeanne de Vionnet, we feel that this is not the way that Charlotte should be married. Though passion of a kind – the passion for acquisition – goes into her capture, she is seen not even as an art object, like the 'extraordinary set of oriental tiles' that Adam Verver acquires at the same time, but as a convenience. However, where Jeanne was both vulnerable and passive, Charlotte brings to her marriage not only the courage and cleverness for which Maggie admires her, but also a devious purpose and a powerful will.

It is at this point that we have to consider the story of Medea. Having used her magic powers, besides her considerable capacity for deception and cruelty, to enable Jason to win the golden fleece, she returns with him to his native city of Iolchus where she becomes his wife; but as a foreigner she has no legal claim on him, and he deserts her for an advantageous marriage with the king's daughter. Charlotte has already been obliged to accept this Medea fate once, when the Prince 'forgets' her for Maggie the millionaire's daughter.

He *had* to have money – it was a question of life and death. It wouldn't have been a bit amusing, either, to marry him as a pauper.
                                                    (Bk 1 ch. 4)

However, when she finds that she is expected also to sacrifice to Maggie her status as Adam Verver's wife and the mistress of his house, she decides to exert her power over the Prince in earnest. At this point in the novel most of our sympathies are with Charlotte. If the Ververs have inadvertently married a pair of former lovers, Charlotte and the Prince have done the same, and Charlotte's sense of the unnaturalness of Maggie's exclusive bond with her father is shared by the more detached Mrs Assingham:

She dresses really, Maggie does, as much for her father – and she always did – as for her husband or for herself. She has her room in his house very much as she had it before she was married – and just as the boy has quite a second nursery there, in which Mrs Noble, when she comes with him, makes herself, I assure you, at home. *Si bien* that if Charlotte, in her own house, so to speak, should wish a friend or two to stay with her, she really would be scarce able to put them up.'

(Bk III ch. 10)

Maggie's attempt to free herself has somehow led to her becoming more than ever her father's wife, and Mrs Assingham gives us a glimpse of the reason – 'It could be that she's unhappy and that she takes her funny little way of consoling herself.' In fact, the tragic action has already become a self-generating system. Maggie's dim and unfocused sense that something is wrong with her world causes her to draw ever nearer to her father and thus to put an ever-increasing pressure on Charlotte to draw nearer to the Prince, who is receptive to her advances, if for no other reason than from sheer boredom – he is, as Colonel Assingham remarks, 'in a position in which he has nothing in life to do' – until the inevitable moment when the sexual tension that has built up between the former lovers demands to be released:

Then of a sudden, through this tightened circle, as at the issue of a narrow strait into the sea beyond, everything broke up, broke down, gave way, melted and mingled. Their lips sought their lips, their pressure their response and their response their pressure; with a violence that had sighed itself the next moment to the longest and deepest of stillnesses they passionately sealed their pledge.

(Bk III ch. 5)

Notice here the use of the sea as a sexual metaphor, and notice too that – like Kate Croy being 'generous' to Milly Theale – the lovers choose to regard their deception of the Ververs, fuelled though it is, in Charlotte's case at least, by jealousy and rage, as 'a conscious care' for them. And indeed they do intend to be careful. There is no need for the sweet and simple creatures they have married ever to suspect.

That first passionate kiss is a pledge that demands a consummation, and the opportunity for it comes soon enough – is provided for them, indeed, as they do not sufficiently stop to consider, by Maggie and her father. The visit to Matcham, from which the Ververs rather oddly cry off at the last moment, takes us to a house that we have already entered with Milly Theale. Somewhere inside it hangs the Bronzino. For Charlotte and the Prince it offers both the chance and the impossibility of being together. James expresses their predicament in yet another flawed erotic moment:

They had found a minute together in the great hall of the house during the half-hour before dinner; this easiest of chances they had already a couple of times arrived at by waiting persistently till the last other loiterers had gone to dress and by being prepared themselves to dress so expeditiously that they might a little later on be among the first to appear in festal array. The hall then was empty, before the army of rearranging cushion-patting housemaids were marshalled in, and there was a place by the forsaken fire, at one end, where they might imitate with art the unpremeditated. Above all here, for the snatched instants, they could breathe so near to each other that the interval was almost engulfed in it and the intensity both of the union and the caution became a workable substitute for contact. They had prolongations of instants that counted as visions of bliss; they had slow approximations that counted as long caresses.   (Bk III ch. 8)

It is a passage that recalls Donne's motionless lovers in their ecstasy of stasis:

> And whilst our souls negotiate there,
>   We like sepulchral statues lay;
> All day, the same our postures were,
>   And we said nothing, all the day
>
> (*The Ecstasy*)

and yet it is shot through with the language of calculation – 'imitate with art', 'caution', 'a workable substitute', 'counted' – as the intensity of their union expresses itself through the shared need to escape not from the moral disapproval but from the avid curiosity of their fellow guests and from the prying eyes of housemaids.

Deception already seems to them the natural air to breathe, and Charlotte's ingenious plan for a day of 'sight-seeing' in Gloucester, a day which will at last enable them to consummate their intensely cautious union, takes them beyond deception into sordid complicity, with its dependence on a crafty, unspoken pact with the adulterous Lady Castleford:

She had detained Charlotte because she wished to detain Mr Blint, and she couldn't detain Mr Blint, disposed though he clearly was to oblige her, without spreading over the act some ampler drapery.

(Bk III ch. 9)

'The act' that Lady Castleford wants to perform with 'sleek civil accomplished' Mr Blint, an act of vulgar, loveless fornication, taints in advance the embrace that we never see in the bedroom of an inn in Gloucester. But that day in Gloucester takes the lovers beyond deception in another sense also. Maggie is not after all so 'very, very simple'. It is a masterstroke of chilling realism that she does not find out what has happened – she *knows*. We first see the effect of this through the appalled and fascinated eyes of match-making, meddling Mrs Assingham:

'It's when one sees people who always *are* natural making little pale pathetic blinking efforts for it – then it is that one knows something's the matter'   (Bk III ch. 11)

but the second half of the novel is to take us inside Maggie's mind, not the mind of a 'little pale pathetic blinking' creature but the arena where a silent and terrible drama is to be played out, the struggle for survival and dominance of a woman who refuses to be a victim. It is as if the ghosts of Catherine Sloper and of Milly Theale were stirring in their graves and rising up against their oppressors. Maggie, the dull little princess, is no longer the king's daughter. Now she is Medea.

We will not understand what happens next unless we realize the full horror of Maggie's now conscious knowledge,

the horror of finding evil seated all at its ease where she had only dreamed of good; the horror of the thing hideously *behind*, behind so much trusted, so much pretended, nobleness, cleverness, tenderness.

(Bk V ch. 2)

Critics have often tried to sweep this horror away with bland formulations which reduce the novel to an etiolated *exercice de style*. For Walter Wright, for example, 'the very worst, the most shocking, experience that Maggie can suffer' is 'knowledge of her husband's adultery, not necessarily in the legal sense, but in the realm of the affections'. What Maggie actually suffers, of course, is the knowledge, unprovable but certain, and insidious as madness, that her husband is sexually involved with her father's wife. The horror is not merely adultery but incest, with its perversion of all relationships, son-in-law and mother-in-law, husband and wife, friend and friend – even father and daughter, for the impossibility of telling what she knows turns the one person left that she can trust into the one she has to lie to. It is this unthinkable complex of false relationships that has lain beneath the smiling surface of her life – and that still lies there, for the smiles go on as Amerigo tries to cover up his tell-tale moment of blank embarrassment:

> he had advanced upon her smiling and smiling, and thus, without hesitation at the last, had taken her into his arms. The hesitation had been at the first...   (Bk IV ch. 1)

the hesitation that has already made it plain to Maggie that all her suspicions are true.

In an astonishing and beautiful moment near the end of *The Tempest*, Miranda and Ferdinand are discovered playing chess, that game symbolic of all corrupt worldly power-struggles, and, in the untarnishable certainty that her words can never come true, Miranda exclaims, 'Sweet lord, you play me false.' Donne expresses the same certainty in the same way:

> Who is so safe as we? where none can do
> Treason to us, except one of us two.
>
> (*The Anniversary*)

When Maggie–Miranda, the Maggie who 'wasn't born to know evil', gaily teases her husband by telling him 'that she never admired him so much, or so found him heart-breakingly handsome, clever, irresistible, in the very degree in which he had originally and fatally dawned upon her, as when she saw other women reduced to the same passive pulp', so that 'even should he some day get drunk and beat her, the spectacle of him with hated rivals' would always 'keep her in love with him', we do not marvel at her trust but anticipate the destruction of her fragile ignorance. In fact she is a Miranda who from her childhood has always been afraid. 'I live in terror', she tells her father. 'I'm a small creeping thing.' When her island changes to the great black house of the Greek tragedy, this image of a frightened animal changes too. Medea destroys the king's daughter by sending her a poisoned wedding-dress. Charlotte–Medea has revenged herself on Maggie by wrapping her marriage in poisoned security, and now it is as the king's daughter that Maggie dresses herself in her 'stiff and grand' new frock, but as she sits waiting for her husband's return, 'her little crouching posture... that of a timid tigress' tells us that now she is a frightened animal that could kill a man. In the course of that patient vigil she changes rôles with Charlotte. It is now Maggie who is cheated, abandoned, betrayed, but instead of feeling sympathy for her, or even pity, we are appalled by the force that has taken possession of her, an obsessive certainty that only differs from madness in that the nightmare it summons up is true. Amerigo tries to lull the nightmare back into a dream and return her to the delusive safety of the island through the only power he has over her, that of his sexuality, but though Maggie sinks, in his embrace, 'under the dizzying smothering welter – positively in submarine depths where everything came to her through walls of emerald and mother-of-pearl', he cannot drown her Medea knowledge. Maggie, who once thought of love as a cruise on a luxury liner, is now submerged in a sea that could turn her bones to coral, not the metamorphic sea that Ariel sang of, the sea that washed the shores of Prospero's island, but the dangerous sea that brought Jason to Colchis' strand.

This image not only establishes the connection in the novel between sexuality and the sea, it also illustrates the effect of barely tolerable pressure on the workings of Maggie's mind. In the early part of the novel we see that she is fanciful and enjoys elaborating extended metaphors. Now, forced to think intensely about the unthinkable, she develops a visionary faculty which enables her to grasp her predicament. It is a common experience, on finding that we have been deceived by someone close to us, to feel, overwhelmingly, 'I don't understand.' It is by the means of vivid and almost hallucinatory mental images that Maggie succeeds in mastering, and thus eventually making use of, her new-found knowledge. When Bernard Shaw wrote his play *Saint Joan*, he needed his heroine to be a practical early protestant, not a catholic mystic. He solved the problem by making Joan:

what Francis Galton and other modern investigators of human faculty call a visualizer. She saw imaginary saints just as some other people see imaginary diagrams and landscapes with numbers dotted about them, and are thereby able to perform feats of memory and arithmetic impossible to non-visualizers. Visualizers will understand this at once. Non-visualizers who have never read Galton will be puzzled and incredulous. But a very little inquiry among their acquaintances will reveal to them that the mind's eye is more or less a magic lantern, and that the street is full of normally sane people who have hallucinations of all sorts which they believe to be part of the normal permanent equipment of all human beings.   (Preface)

Galton's *Inquiries into Human Faculty and its Development* was first published in 1883. In it he recounts the rather surprising results of a piece of straightforward research. A questionnaire on 'the illumination, definition, and colouring of the mental image' elicited baffled and sceptical replies from the fellow scientists on whom he first tried it, but:

when I spoke to persons whom I met in general society, I found an entirely different disposition to prevail. Many men and a yet larger number of women, and many boys and girls, declared that they habitually saw mental imagery, and that it was perfectly distinct to them and full of colour. The more I pressed and cross-questioned them, professing myself to be incredulous, the more obvious was the truth of their first assertions. They described their imagery in minute detail, and they spoke in a tone of surprise at my apparent hesitation in accepting what they said. I felt that I myself should have spoken exactly as they did if I had been describing a scene that lay before my eyes, in broad daylight, to a blind man who persisted in doubting the reality of vision.

James, unlike Shaw, was not a writer with a scientific bent. Though the twenty years that separated the publication of Galton's book from the writing of *The Golden Bowl* would have been sufficient for the diffusion of Galton's findings into the common knowledge of educated people, it is just as likely that

James endowed Maggie with this visualizing faculty because he possessed it himself. Either way, he uses it, unlike Shaw, for wholly poetic purposes. From that first extraordinary image of a great pagoda rearing itself in the 'very centre of the garden of her life', a structure that embodies her sense that a sinister secret is being hidden behind a 'decorated surface', Maggie's visions dominate the second half of the book. Sometimes the effect is a kind of phantasmagoria, as when she turns her imagination on the mystery of her husband's relationship with his mistress:

This was a realm it could people with images – again and again with fresh ones; they swarmed there like the strange combinations that lurked in the woods at twilight; they loomed into the definite and faded into the vague, their main present sign for her being however that they were always, that they were duskily, agitated.

(Bk v ch. 4)

Sometimes, and alarmingly, like Joan's more rational visions, they re-enact themselves in real life. Her imaginary cardgame – 'there was a card she could play, but there was only one, and to play it would be to end the game' – resolves into the scene where she walks round the bridge-table at Fawns with 'the green cloth and the silver flambeaux', looking at each of the players in turn and knowing that 'she might sound out their doom in a single sentence'. But images are not merely creations of the mind, they are also the code we use to read the world, and the most potent image of the novel comes not out of Maggie's head but into her hands. At the centre of the novel the golden bowl, first whole and then shattered, lies like a ritual object on the shelf above Maggie's hearth.

It is when she acquires the golden bowl that Maggie begins to have power over her life. Mrs Assingham, whose initial scepticism about the significance of the bowl – 'the gilt cup', as she calls it – is a last desperate attempt to disown her complicity with Amerigo and Charlotte, is turned into the priestess who must ritually destroy it:

So for an instant, full of her thought and of her act, she held the precious vessel, and then with due note taken of the margin of the polished floor, bare fine and hard in the embrasure of her window, dashed it boldly to the ground.   (Bk IV ch. 9)

The Prince, summoned by her act, is exposed, for all his blankly urbane attempts to keep his head, as a liar and even as a fool:

leaving Maggie to feel as in a flash how such a consequence, a foredoomed infelicity, partaking of the ridiculous even in one of the cleverest, might be of the very essence of the penalty of wrong-doing.   (Bk IV ch. 10)

But though the bowl gives Maggie a new power, it also defines her powerlessness. It breaks into three pieces but Maggie can 'carry but two of the fragments at once'. It is her turn now to perform a ritual act:

She brought them over to the chimney-piece, to the conspicuous place occupied by the cup before Fanny's appropriation of it, and after laying them carefully down went back for what remained, the solid detached foot. With this she returned to the mantel-shelf, placing it with deliberation in the centre and then for a minute occupying herself as with the attempt to fit the other morsels together. The split determined by the latent crack was so sharp and so neat that if there had been anything to hold them the bowl might still quite beautifully, a few steps away, have passed for uninjured. As there was however nothing to hold them but Maggie's hands during the few moments the latter were so employed, she could only lay the almost equal parts of the vessel carefully beside their pedestal and leave them thus before her husband's eyes.   (Bk IV ch. 10)

   This fairy-tale attempt to pick up and piece together the 'formless fragments' of the golden bowl and so restore it to what it had never really been – 'The bowl with all our happiness in it. The bowl without the crack' – is to occupy Maggie for the rest of the novel. The task brings with it another change of rôle. The power generated by the breaking of the bowl has enabled Maggie to defeat Amerigo, but now she faces her real adversary. Deserted by her lover, who does his best to convince her that Maggie knows nothing, and suspected by her husband, Charlotte is now fighting for her life, a fight that she can win only by reducing Maggie–Medea to the little princess in a fairy-tale, victim of a cruel stepmother with the power to poison her father's mind against her. Maggie has one card, which she can only play at the price of ending the game, and now Charlotte threatens to play it first by telling Adam Verver that his daughter, eaten up by irrational jealousy, has invented a monstrous story about her father's wife. This threat, unspoken but menacing, is acted out in the scene on the terrace which follows the game of bridge at which Maggie fails to play her one card.

This new danger has arisen just as Maggie has begun to feel a wary pity for Charlotte's caged and tormented state:

The cage was the deluded condition, and Maggie, as having known delusion – rather! – understood the nature of cages   (Bk v ch. 1)

but when the cage door opens suddenly 'from within', the piteous bird, beating its 'bruised wings' against the 'gilt wires', is transformed into a 'splendid shining supple creature', a great cat 'escaped by force' from its captivity. It is hardly a metaphor. Maggie shrinks in real terror from the tigress that stalks her round the dark terrace. The spring of the hunting beast comes in a falsely reproachful question.

'Have you any ground of complaint of me? Is there any wrong you consider I've done you? I feel at last that I've a right to ask you.'
(Bk v ch. 2)

Now it is Maggie who is trapped as Charlotte ruthlessly presses her question home, though she manages to express her condemnation even as she acknowledges her powerlessness to pursue it.

'I accuse you – I accuse you of nothing.'

It appears to be a moment of total defeat, and yet, even as she speaks, Maggie has a foretaste of victory. The lie that she has been bullied into telling is the lie that Amerigo has already told:

They were together thus, he and she, close, close together – whereas Charlotte, though rising there radiantly before her, was really off in some darkness of space that would steep her in solitude and harass her with care. The heart of the Princess swelled accordingly even in her abasement; she had kept in tune with the right, and something certainly, something that might resemble a rare flower snatched from an impossible ledge, would, and possibly soon, come of it for her.

(Bk v ch. 2)

Charlotte, at this point, of course, believes that she has won. It is when she underlines her victory by saying, Judas-like, 'Will you kiss me on it then', that she loses our last shred of sympathy. This final taunt is a kind of blasphemy; but though it leaves Maggie unable to speak it also makes her realize 'how much too far Charlotte had come to retreat'. The 'shining supple creature' has been 'hemmed in and secured' after all. She has locked herself into the fiction that nothing has occurred.

Maggie has fought on her stepmother's terms and won through the fairy-tale weapons of humility and patience (this was why James had to make her a princess) but she would have had to lay down her Medea rôle in any case. The fierce Medea emotions, 'the straight vindictive view, the rights of resentment, the rages of jealousy, the protests of passion', have passed her by like

a wild eastern caravan, looming into view with crude colours in the sun, fierce pipes in the air, high spears against the sky, all a thrill, a natural joy to mingle with, but turning off short before it reached her and plunging into other defiles.   (Bk v ch. 2)

Maggie can understand what it would mean to lose herself, maenad-like, in the savage pleasures of revenge, but it is not for her. Medea avenges herself on her faithless husband in the most terrible way possible – by killing her children – but Maggie still feels for Amerigo 'the hard little passion which nothing he had done could smother'. In any case, her father sits guarding the Principino's bed 'with eyes apparently closed'. No longer Medea, Maggie reverts to her natural rôle, Miranda the magician's daughter. This return to Prospero's island is accompanied, not surprisingly, by sea imagery. Maggie's earlier attempt to repeat Miranda's paradoxical profession of trust, 'Sweet lord, you play me false', had been undermined by her ignorance of Amerigo's true nature. Now she tells her father what her suffering has taught her about love:

'My idea is this, that when you only love a little you're naturally not jealous – or are only jealous also a little, so that it doesn't matter. But when you love in a deeper and intenser way, then you're in the very same proportion jealous; your jealousy has intensity and, no doubt, ferocity. When however you love in the most abysmal and unutterable way of all – why then you're beyond everything, and nothing can pull you down.' (Bk v ch. 3)

Earlier, Amerigo's embrace had threatened her with drowning. Now her father sees her as

a creature consciously floating and shining in a warm summer sea, some element of dazzling sapphire and silver, a creature cradled upon depths, buoyant among dangers, in which fear or folly or sinking otherwise than in play was impossible. (Bk v ch. 3)

For the only time, James gives us a vision of human sexuality as pure delight, but the vision is not of what Maggie possesses but of what Adam Verver implacably wants for his daughter. Maggie has only indirectly been countering the accusation that Charlotte has threatened to make, the accusation of irrational jealousy, but both father and daughter understand the unspoken subtext of their conversation. Adam Verver's proposal to take Charlotte back to American City affects Maggie like

a blur of light in the midst of which she saw Charlotte like some object marked by contrast in blackness, saw her waver in the field of vision, saw her removed, transported, doomed. (Bk v ch. 3)

The stern embrace which follows seals their unspoken compact, their mutual acquiescence in Charlotte's doom and its necessary consequence, their loss of each other.

As with Maggie's terrible realization, it is necessary to understand the full horror of Charlotte's doom, which has been seen by some critics, following the lead of F. R. Leavis, as simply a matter of having to live in American City, considered by James, they assume, to be a 'penal settlement'. While it is certainly true that James would no more have wanted to spend his own life in a brash, raw, cultureless far western city than would, if they were honest, his critics themselves, this in no way accounts for the endless torment to which Charlotte is condemned. She has been abandoned without a word by her lover, from whom she is now to be parted for ever – Maggie, well placed to understand the pain of this, sees her as 'doomed to a separation that was like a knife in her heart' – and is now to be led into an exile that she can neither resist nor question by a husband who will never allow her either to forget, or to be entirely certain whether he knows about, the terrible thing she has done. She is to spend her days in captivity in Adam Verver's 'museum of museums', not even as an exhibit but as the servant of the treasures, a rôle for which he is already implacably training her.

As she shows off the beauties of the collection to parties of visitors to Fawns, Charlotte is made to describe her own captive state:

'The largest of the three pieces has the rare peculiarity that the garlands looped round it, which as you see are the finest possible *vieux Saxe*, aren't of the same origin or period, or even, wonderful as they are, of a taste quite so perfect. They've been put on at a later time by a process known through very few examples, and through none so important as this, which is really quite unique – so that though the whole thing is a little *baroque* its value as a specimen is I believe almost inestimable.'   (Bk v ch. 4)

'The garlands looped round it' have 'been put on at a later time'. Maggie, the visualizer, can see and hear what the visitors only uneasily sense – the 'small perpetual hum of contemplation' which comes from her father 'as if he were singing to himself, *sotto voce*, as he went' and the result of the spell that he is weaving, the 'long silken halter' looped round Charlotte's beautiful neck:

He didn't twitch it, yet it was there; he didn't drag her, but she came.   (Bk v ch. 4)

Overcome with pity at what only her ears and her father's can hear, 'the shriek of a soul in pain', Maggie turns to the window and sees 'the lighted square before her all blurred and dim', like that 'blur of light' against which she had seen Charlotte's doomed silhouette. When she looks at her father she sees that his eyes too are full of 'strange tears'. He understands, just as

Maggie does, the full cruelty of what he is doing to Charlotte, and he will never relent.

At the end of *The Tempest*, Shakespeare contrasts Prospero's formal profession of forgiveness to the brother who has injured and still hates him:

> For you, most wicked sir, whom to call brother
> Would even infect my mouth, I do forgive
> Thy rankest fault

> (Act V Sc. 1)

with the true forgiveness which, paradoxically, can never be expressed because the goodwill of the wronged and the grief of the wrong-doer have between them cancelled out the wrong:

> There, sir, stop.
> Let us not burden our remembrance with
> A heaviness that's gone.

Adam Verver, by contrast, is a Prospero who can pity but cannot forgive his victim, a magician who can never break his staff and abjure his magic. Instead it is left to Maggie to make the attempt at forgiveness. Maggie has already ceased to see herself as the heroine of the tragedy; not only the fury but even the horror of Medea's plight have 'almost failed her', though she is still aware of the inevitability of the tragic action in which all four actors are bound to maintain the 'equilibrium' which is their common doom. There are even moments when the dark forces that control the action become apparent to her. The evening of the bridge game that culminates in Charlotte's Judas kiss seems to her 'a thing appointed by some occult power'. Now, though, it is Charlotte that she sees as the tragic heroine of 'an ancient fable', 'some vision of Io goaded by the gadfly or of Ariadne roaming the lone sea-strand'. In a scene that is the mirror-image of the night-time encounter on the terrace, she pursues Charlotte into the mid-day heat of the garden. As with the terrace scene, the architecture of the garden externalizes the psychological predicament of the characters, with its long perspectives 'converging in separate green vistas at a sort of umbrageous temple, an ancient rotunda, pillared and statued', where Charlotte has taken refuge. Charlotte has been driven into the centre of the labyrinth and now she sees her enemy approaching down one of the long vistas, an enemy who comes unarmed and in friendship to deliver a message of peace:

'I saw you come out – saw you from my window and couldn't bear to think you should find yourself here without the beginning of your book. *This* is the beginning; you've got the wrong volume and I've brought you out the right.' (Bk v ch. 5)

It is the answer, if only Charlotte would take it, to the problem of fitting together the pieces of the golden bowl. If the broken shards become the three volumes of a novel, all that is needed is to start at the beginning again and read them in the right order. But Charlotte, pitiful and driven as she seems to Maggie, still has all Medea's furious pride. Rather than accept Maggie's offer of forgiveness, she claims her own impending exile as a successful bid to remove her husband from his daughter's jealous clutches. Maggie, who has come out into the garden to help and befriend Charlotte, is given instead the chance to be rid of her for ever. As in the scene on the terrace, she needs only to play Charlotte's game and by pretending to lose she will become the winner. Only one deceitful sentence is needed and with a 'sharp, successful, almost primitive wail' she utters it:

'You want to take my father *from* me?'

Before Charlotte walks away, 'splendid and erect', 'down the long vista', Maggie takes up the two volumes of the novel and lays them down together. She has defeated Charlotte but the story is not yet over. There is still the third volume of the novel, the third piece of the bowl, the last act in the tragedy.

Maggie's problem with Amerigo is not how to forgive him; she has already done so. In a beautiful image, James shows her converting the bitterness of her suffering into sweetness:

There were hours enough, lonely hours, in which she let dignity go; then there were others when, clinging with her winged concentration to some deep cell of her heart, she stored away her hived tenderness as if she had gathered it all from flowers. (Bk v ch. 4)

However, in order to taste the fruit of her victory she must free him from the prison in which he has wilfully incarcerated himself, and this she cannot do until her father and Charlotte are gone. As she waits, in the stagnant emptiness of a London August, for the final ritual of farewell, she is still haunted by the thought of Charlotte. Could she not do one last thing for her, give her the chance of a few hours alone with Amerigo, hours which, like the original expedition to find the golden bowl, would be a *ricordo*, something to be

carried away into exile like the last saved object of price of the *émigré*, the jewel wrapped in a piece of old silk and negotiable some day in the market of misery. (Bk VI ch. 1)

This fantasy of magnanimity, with its underlying purpose of forcing Amerigo to face up, at last, to what he has done to Charlotte, trapped in real earnest while he lurks in his 'monastic cell' 'by his own act and his own choice', is checked by the compelling image of her father:

The thing that never failed now as an item in the picture was that gleam of the silken noose, his wife's immaterial tether, so marked to Maggie's sense during her last month in the country. Mrs Verver's straight neck had certainly not slipped it; nor had the other end of the long cord – oh quite conveniently long! – disengaged its smaller loop from the hooked thumb that, with his fingers closed upon it, her husband kept out of sight. To have recognized, for all its tenuity, the play of this gathered lasso might inevitably be to wonder with what magic it was twisted, to what tension subjected, but could never be to doubt either of its adequacy to its office or of its perfect durability. (Bk VI ch.1)

Charlotte, who has never been told about the return of the golden bowl into the story, has become its slave; she could only be freed from this captivity by being freed from her ignorance, which is, as Maggie asserts with tears like her father's in her eyes, 'a torment'. But for all Maggie's pity, she is now as implacable as her father. When Amerigo suggests that he might tell Charlotte the truth, Maggie replies, with 'the very first clear majesty he had known her to use', 'Aren't you rather forgetting who she is?' Aren't you forgetting, she means, of course, that Charlotte is my father's wife. She must be left to the pride that is at once her armour and her punishment.

Amerigo, for his part, and despite his captive state, is disinclined to suffer – for Charlotte or for anyone else – more than he has to. His 'Everything's terrible, cara – in the heart of man', though it sums up the tragedy, is a wisdom inherited with the dark traditions of his family, a knowledge innate and therefore easy to bear, where for Maggie, who has learnt it with such effort and pain, and indeed for Charlotte, 'condemned after a couple of short years to find the golden flame – oh the golden flame! – a mere handful of black ashes', it is a felt and lived reality. Once again he tries to exert his sexual power over Maggie:

She had, with her hand still on the knob, her back against the door, so that her retreat under his approach must be less than a step, and yet she couldn't for her life with the other hand have pushed him away. He was so near now that she could touch him, taste him, smell him, hold him; he almost pressed upon her, and the warmth of his face – frowning, smiling, she mightn't know which; only beautiful and strange – was bent upon her with the largeness with which objects loom in dreams.   (Bk vi ch. 2)

Nothing is left of the shipwrecked luxury liner on which she began her marriage journey but a single plank, yet it suffices to keep her for a little longer from the final plunge into 'the great sea'. She cannot abandon herself to its waters until the final act is played out.

The farewell visit of her father and Charlotte, round which she has woven such fantasy plans, turns out to be a cold formality. Father and daughter have already said their real farewells in that 'august and almost stern' embrace in the garden at Fawns. The meeting yields only a chilling reminder of the motivation that lay behind both their marriages, as we see Charlotte and the Prince once again reduced to art objects:

The fusion of their presence with the decorative elements, their contribution to the triumph of selection, was complete and admirable; though to a lingering view, a view more penetrating than the occasion really demanded, they also might have figured as concrete attestations of a rare power of purchase.   (Bk vi ch. 3)

All Maggie's attempts to forgive Charlotte end simply in the declaration that she is indeed 'incomparable' – a piece worth her purchase price, and to be valued at last because that price has turned out to be so high.

At the very end of the book, Maggie stands alone on the balcony and waits for a price of another sort – 'the golden fruit that had shone from afar'. Now, if ever, she is to receive what she has struggled for: 'The bowl with all our happiness in it. The bowl without the crack.' At the end of a tragedy, the spectators should feel pity and fear, but what emotions are they left with when it is the protagonist that feels so. The true horror of the tragedy lies in its happy ending. As Amerigo, with shining eyes, exclaims, '"See"'? I see nothing but *you*', Maggie, for pity and dread of this appalling truth, blinds her own eyes by burying her face in his breast. For the second time Amerigo has not only abandoned Charlotte, he has obliterated all memory of her. The story ends here, because it must. Our imaginations can pursue it no further.

In his preface to *The Golden Bowl* in the New York edition, James speaks of the true nature of poetry:

The seer and speaker under the descent of the god is the 'poet', whatever his form, and he ceases to be one only when his form, whatever else it may nominally or superficially or vulgarly be, is unworthy of the god.

Perhaps the only emotion left to the spectators when the tragedy has pushed them beyond pity and dread is awe as the power of the god departs from the seer whose own powers have been able to sustain the tragedy to its unforeseen, inevitable end.

CHAPTER 9

Afterword

A novelist is more than his novels, and I would like to end this book by giving you a glimpse of the man himself. This is not altogether easy to do – the well-known collection of not quite affectionate little anecdotes which pretend to tell us what he was like were all produced by wicked verbal cartoonists – Max Beerbohm, Edith Wharton, Virginia Woolf – who shared a talent for making a good story better. Leon Edel, James's biographer, suggests that in old age James came to resemble Dr Johnson in manner and bearing, and this analogy can be taken further. As with Johnson, it is impossible to read a great deal about James without feeling an enormous affection for him. Like Johnson's, his personality is unmistakable yet hard to sum up except in paradoxes – he was sociable but intensely solitary, reserved yet effusively affectionate, neurotic but enormously sane. Like Johnson, our sense of him is made up of the stories about him, and yet a thousand stories would not suffice to contain him.

I wish I could include all the thousand stories here, but there is space only for one. Virginia Woolf, in her biography of Roger Fry, describes how James several times visited the second Post-Impressionist Exhibition of 1912 and, as an old friend of the organizer, would be taken by Fry

down to the basement where, among the packing cases and the brown paper, tea would be provided. Seated on a little hard chair, Henry James would express 'in convoluted sentences the disturbed hesitations which Matisse and Picasso aroused in him, and Roger Fry, exquisitely, with something of the old-world courtesy which James carried about with him', would do his best to convey to the great novelist what he meant by saying that Cézanne and Flaubert were, in a manner of speaking, after the same thing. (ch. 7, s. v)

Randall Jarrell once painted a memorable picture of Charlemagne, the great emperor of the Holy Roman Empire, struggling and failing as an old man to make himself literate. For Jarrell, his 'absurd vision of the white-bearded king trying to learn to read, running his big finger slowly along under the words', was a touchstone for the value of the culture that he himself was battling to defend in philistine modern America. The picture of the great novelist, in his seventieth year and with *The Golden Bowl* already behind him, struggling with only partial success to understand and appreciate Picasso has the same nobility and pathos.

When Jarrell died, his friend and fellow poet John Berryman spoke of meeting him again 'in the chambers of the end'; and it was in the chambers of the end, a phantasmagoria of panelled rooms that was at one and the same time the Reform Club and the halls of the Underworld, that another American poet, Ezra Pound, encountered in imagination the ghost of Henry James:

> And the great domed head, *con gli occhi onesti e*
> > *tardi*
> Moves before me, phantom with weighted motion,
> *Grave incessu*, drinking the tone of things,
> And the old voice lifts itself
> > weaving an endless sentence.

(canto VII)

James himself, at the end of an evening spent delightedly reading Walt Whitman aloud to Edith Wharton, threw up his hands and exclaimed, 'Undoubtedly a very great genius! Only one cannot help deploring his too-extensive acquaintance with the foreign languages.' Here Pound translates the Latin for us – *grave incessu*, with weighted motion. The Italian, which he quotes from memory, comes from Dante's *Purgatorio* and means 'with dignified, slow eyes'.

There are many contemporary witnesses to the penetrating power of James's remarkable eyes. They still look out at us, from Matthew Brady's daguerreotype of the serious small boy

standing shyly with his hand on his father's shoulder as from
John Singer Sargent's famous portrait of the 70-year-old great
man. E. H. Gombrich, in 'The Mask and the Face: the
Perception of Physiognomic Likeness in Life and in Art', puts
together two photographs of Bertrand Russell, as a small child
and as an old man, and says:

It certainly would not be easy to programme a computer to pick out
the invariant, and yet it is the same face.

If we watch ourselves testing this assertion and comparing the two
pictures, we may find that we are probing the face of the child trying
to project into it, or onto it, the more familiar face of the aged
philosopher...his mother, if she could be alive, would look in the
features of the old man for the traces of the child, and having lived
through this slow transformation, would be more likely to succeed.

As we look at the face of the child Henry James, frozen in a
crystalline moment of time with his long future before him, we
realize that in the end he is unknowable. Human personality is
a mystery that not all the toils of the biographer can plumb,
and yet the writer of great imaginative fiction can illuminate it
for us in an instant, 'in the twinkling of an eye'. The little
fragment of Dante that Pound quotes comes from Virgil's
meeting on the slopes of Mount Purgatory with the poet
Sordello. Discovering that they are citizens of the same city,
and completely forgetting that they are bodiless ghosts in a
narrative famous for its science-fiction realism, joyfully they
embrace each other.

Select bibliography

JAMES'S NOVELS

Watch and Ward (1871)
Roderick Hudson (1875)
The American (1877)
The Europeans (1878)
Confidence (1880)
Washington Square (1881)
The Portrait of a Lady (1881)
The Bostonians (1886)
The Princess Casamassima (1886)
The Reverberator (1888)
The Tragic Muse (1890)
The Other House (1896)
The Spoils of Poynton (1897)
What Maisie Knew (1897)
The Awkward Age (1899)
The Sacred Fount (1901)
The Wings of the Dove (1902)
The Ambassadors (1903)
The Golden Bowl (1904)

(Note: *The Ambassadors* was completed before *The Wings of the Dove* but published later; I have discussed these two novels in order of composition.)

UNFINISHED NOVELS

The Ivory Tower (1917)
The Sense of the Past (1917)

SHORT STORIES

The Complete Tales of Henry James, 12 vols., edited by Leon Edel, Hart-Davis, 1962–4

James revised what he saw as his best fiction for the 24-volume New York edition of *The Novels and Tales of Henry James*, Charles Scribner and Sons, 1907–9. This omitted much of his work, including *The Europeans, Washington Square* and *The Bostonians.*

PLAYS

The Complete Plays of Henry James, edited by Leon Edel, Hart-Davis, 1949

AUTOBIOGRAPHY

A Small Boy and Others (1913)
Notes of a Son and Brother (1914)
The Middle Years (1917)

Collected in *Henry James: Autobiography*, edited by F. W. Dupee, Criterion Books, 1956

CRITICISM

French Poets and Novelists (1878)
Hawthorne (1879)
Partial Portraits (1888)
Notes on Novelists (1914)
The Painter's Eye, edited by John L. Sweeney, Hart-Davis, 1956

TRAVEL BOOKS

A Little Tour in France (1900)
English Hours (1905)
The American Scene (1907)
Italian Hours (1909)

LETTERS AND NOTEBOOKS

The Letters of Henry James, edited by Percy Lubbock, Macmillan, 1920
Henry James: Letters, edited by Leon Edel, Macmillan, 1974–84
The Complete Notebooks of Henry James, edited by Leon Edel and Lyall H. Powers, Oxford University Press, 1987

BIBLIOGRAPHIES

For a complete list of James's work, see:

Edel, Leon and Laurence, Dan, *A Bibliography of Henry James*, Hart-Davis, 1957

The New Cambridge Bibliography of English Literature, vol. III, Cambridge University Press, 1969

AUTHORS QUOTED OR REFERRED TO IN THIS BOOK

CRITICS AND BIOGRAPHERS OF JAMES

Edel, Leon, *The Life of Henry James*, Hart-Davis, 1953–72

Forster, E. M., 'The Ambassadors', from *Aspects of the Novel*, reprinted in Leon Edel (ed.), *Henry James, a Collection of Critical Essays*, Prentice-Hall, 1963

Gosse, Edmund, *Aspects and Impressions*, Cassell, 1922

Leavis, F. R., *The Great Tradition*, Chatto and Windus, 1948

Pound, Ezra, 'A Brief Note (1918)', reprinted in Leon Edel (ed.), *Henry James, a Collection of Critical Essays*, Prentice-Hall, 1963

Stewart, J. I. M., *Eight Modern Writers*, Oxford University Press, 1963

Wright, Walter, 'Maggie Verver: Neither Saint nor Witch', reprinted in Tony Tanner (ed.), *Henry James, Modern Judgements*, Macmillan, 1968

OTHER

Anon, *Unprotected Females in Norway; or The Pleasantest Way of Travelling There*, Routledge, 1857

Galton, Francis, *Inquiries into Human Faculty and its Development*, Macmillan, 1883

Gombrich, E. H., 'The Mask and the Face: the Perception of Physiognomic Likeness in Life and in Art', in *Art, Perception, and Reality*, Johns Hopkins University Press, 1972

James, Alice, *The Diary of Alice James*, edited by Leon Edel, Dodd, Mead and Co. Inc., 1964

Jarrell, Randall, 'The Taste of the Age', in *A Sad Heart at the Supermarket*, Atheneum, 1962

Lorenz, Konrad, *King Solomon's Ring*, trans. Marjorie Kerr Wilson, Methuen, 1952

Woolf, Virginia, *Roger Fry: a Biography*, The Hogarth Press, 1940

OTHER BOOKS WHOLLY OR PARTLY ABOUT JAMES

This is only a selection from the enormous body of criticism on James.

Allen, Elizabeth, *A Woman's Place in the Novels of Henry James*, Macmillan, 1984

Anderson, Charles R., *Person, Place and Thing in Henry James's Novels*, Duke University Press, 1977

Berland, Alwyn, *Culture and Conduct in the Novels of Henry James*, Cambridge University Press, 1981

Bewley, Marius, *The Complex Fate: Hawthorne, Henry James and Some Other American Writers*, Chatto and Windus, 1952

Bradbury, Nicola, *Henry James: The Later Novels*, Oxford University Press, 1979

Brooks, Van Wyck, *The Pilgrimage of Henry James*, E. P. Dutton, 1925

Coveney, Peter, 'Innocence in Henry James' in *The Image of Childhood*, rev. edn, Peregrine Books, 1967

Crews, Frederick C., *The Tragedy of Manners: Moral Drama in the Later Novels of Henry James*, Yale University Press, 1957

Dupee, F. W. (ed.), *The Question of Henry James: A Collection of Critical Essays*, Holt, Rinehart and Winston, 1945

Galloway, David, *Henry James: The Portrait of a Lady*, Edward Arnold, 1967

Gard, Roger (ed.), *Henry James: The Critical Heritage*, Routledge, 1968

Gervais, David, *Flaubert and Henry James*, Macmillan, 1978

Goode, John (ed.), *The Air of Reality*, Methuen, 1972

Graham, Kenneth, *Henry James: The Drama of Fulfilment*, Oxford University Press, 1975

  Indirections of the Novel: James, Conrad and Forster, Cambridge University Press, 1988

Grover, Philip, *Henry James and the French Novel*, Elek Books, 1973

Holland, Laurence Bedwell, *The Expense of Vision: Essays on the Craft of Henry James*, Princeton University Press, 1964

Jefferson, D. W., *Henry James and the Modern Reader*, Oliver and Boyd, 1964

Krook, Dorothea, *The Ordeal of Consciousness in Henry James*, Cambridge University Press, 1962

Lebowitz, Naomi, *The Imagination of Loving: Henry James's Legacy to the Novel*, Wayne State University Press, 1965

Matthiessen, F. O., *Henry James: the Major Phase*, Oxford University Press, 1944

  The James Family, Alfred A. Knopf, 1947

Moore, Harry T., *Henry James and His World*, Thames and Hudson, 1974
Putt, S. Gorley, *A Reader's Guide to Henry James*, Thames and Hudson, 1966
   A Preface to Henry James, Longman, 1986
Vann, J. Don (ed.), *Critics on Henry James*, University of Miami Press, 1972
Winner, Viola Hopkins, *Henry James and the Visual Arts*, University Press of Virginia, 1970
Yeazell, Ruth Bernard, *Language and Knowledge in the Late Novels of Henry James*, University of Chicago Press, 1976